Juvenile Instructor Office

Fragments of Experience

designed for the instruction and encouragement of young Latter-day

Saints

Juvenile Instructor Office

Fragments of Experience
designed for the instruction and encouragement of young Latter-day Saints

ISBN/EAN: 9783337335977

Printed in Europe, USA, Canada, Australia, Japan

Cover: Foto ©Lupo / pixelio.de

More available books at **www.hansebooks.com**

FRAGMENTS

O F

EXPERIENCE,

SIXTH BOOK OF THE

FAITH-PROMOTING SERIES.

Designed for the Instruction and Encouragement of
Young Latter-day Saints.

JUVENILE INSTRUCTOR OFFICE,
Salt Lake City,
1882.

PREFACE.

IN issuing this, the Sixth Book of the FAITH-PROMOTING SERIES, we trust that it will meet with the same kind reception that its predecessors have. Perhaps no books that have ever been published in our Church have become so popular in so short a time as the volumes of this Series which have already been issued. They have tended towards supplying a want which has long been felt in our community, and we feel assured that they have done a great amount of good.

Young minds, as a rule, are not attracted by those publications which treat specially upon doctrine. They are usually too profound for young people to grasp and fully comprehend the ideas that are contained in them. To the person with fully matured mind and well-developed reasoning faculties they may appear ever so simple, and even fascinating, but to most young people they are uninteresting, to some positively distasteful. And yet there is scarcely a child but can be taught principle in the form of narrative, wherein the application is made for him in scenes from real life, and appreciate it. There is no more sure way of instilling into the mind of a child faith in God and in the work which He has established upon the earth than by illustrating it with incidents from actual experience. The lesson, too, is likely to be all the more effective in the persons whose lives are held up for examples are those with whom the child is acquainted and in whom he has confidence. The lives of many of the Elders of the Church of Jesus Christ of Latter-day Saints abound in incidents which, if written and published, would tend to inspire those who might read them with faith in God and a spirit of emulation. We hope a more general interest may soon be felt throughout our Church in writing up such incidents. That the host of children now growing' up in the valleys of the mountains appreciate and are ready to profit by their perusal there can be no doubt.

The FRAGMENTS OF EXPERIENCE herein contained are collected at random, but many valuable lessons may be drawn from the incidents narrated, and we trust that the seed which they may sow in the hearts of those who peruse them will be productive of a rich yield of fruit, in the kingdom of our Father.

THE PUBLISHER.

CONTENTS.

HELP FROM THE LORD.

EARLY EXPERIENCE OF A LATTER-DAY SAINT.

DISOBEDIENCE TO COUNSEL.

LORENZO DOW YOUNG'S NARRATIVE.

CHAPTER VI.

AN INSTANCE OF DIVINE INTERPOSITION.

MY LAST MISSION TO THE SANDWICH ISLANDS.

CHAPTER I.

CHAPTER II.

A PROPHECY FULFILLED.

SPECIAL PROVIDENCES.

INCIDENTS ON THE PLAINS.

CHAPTER I.

CHAPTER II.

HELP FROM THE LORD.

By C.

MISSION IN ILLINOIS WHEN A BOY—ATTEMPT OF A DEACON
TO PUT ME TO SHAME—OPEN MY BIBLE TO THE PAS-
SAGE REQUIRED—PROVE OUR POSITION CORRECT FROM
THE SCRIPTURES — BEFRIENDED BY AN INFIDEL —
PREACHER'S ASSAULT ON THE "FROGS"—THE "FROG"
REPLIES.

IN the year 1845, I was appointed on a mission from
Nauvoo, to labor about Cass County, Illinois, in company
with Theodore Curtis.

After traveling together we concluded to separate, and I
continued alone, preaching wherever an opportunity presented
itself.

One evening I was approaching a little town called Vir-
ginia, foot-sore and weary, having been frequently denied
food.

I retired, as was my wont particularly when so impressed,
for prayer, and for God to soften the hearts of those I might
meet, to give me shelter, food and rest, and finally to open up
my way.

Towards evening I found a number of persons congregated
at the country store. I saluted them with "Good-evening,"
and inquired the opportunity of getting a chance to preach in
that place.

I carried the badge of a "Mormon" preacher in my hand,
namely, a small round valise, containing a shirt, change of

1

socks, Bible and hymn book. I was soon assured by one or two that there was no earthly show for a "Mormon" preacher to be heard in that place.

I replied, "I would like to preach in that nice, newly-finished meeting-house just opposite." A man spoke up quite authoritatively, and said that no "Mormon" should preach in that house, which had just been dedicated—I think for Presbyterian worship.

They termed this man the deacon. This produced considerable talk, for many of the crowd were of what is termed the liberal or infidel persuasion, so much so that the deacon was overwhelmed by argument, shame and reproach, for refusing a boy like me a chance to preach.

To cover his shame and to nonplus me, he remarked, "I have heard say that your preachers are pretty apt with the scriptures, and can produce almost any doctrine you like from the Bible." I replied that the men were, but that I was but a boy; yet I thought I knew a little of the scriptures.

He remarked "Your people believe in laying hands on the sick; don't you?"

I answered that we did, and because Christ had said in His remarkable commission to His apostles, that this was one of the signs following, quoting Mark xvi., 15-18. I also quoted James v., 14.

"Yes, yes;" says he, "that is all very good, but that says only once, and your Elders sometimes lay hands twice in succession on the same person. Whoever heard of Jesus or the apostles doing anything like that?" He then cited an instance where, as he said, Joseph Smith had done this in administering to a sick woman.

The good-natured excitement was intense. The deacon thought I was overwhelmed, and proposed that if I could prove a similar transaction from the scriptures, I might preach in that house that very night.

Eagerness now seized the men, and the deacon chuckled over his presumed victory, and boasted of his acquaintance with the "Blessed Word."

I unbuckled my valise, drew forth my little Bible, and opened it intuitively to this passage in Mark viii., 22-25:

"And he cometh to Bethsaida; and they bring a blind man unto him, and besought him to touch him. And he took the blind man by the hand, * * * and put his hands upon him, and asked him if he saw aught. And he looked up, and said, I see men as trees, walking. After that he put his hands *again* upon his eyes, and made him·look up: and he was restored, and saw every man clearly."

The reading of this scripture; the sudden finding of it, for I was led to it as clearly as a man leads his horse to the water; its aptness and conclusiveness, accompanied by the jeers of the infidel portion of the crowd, mortified the deacon—he was discomfited.

I remarked that I would, according to the deacon's terms, preach in the church that evening, provided some one would find candles. The candles were instantly offered, and accordingly, I preached with power and the demonstration of the Spirit.

After the close of the services, I found a resting place with one of the most avowed infidels of the neighborhood, who had listened to the talk between the deacon and myself, and who particularly enjoyed the good man's discomfiture. By his persuasion I staid some time in the neighborhood, occupying occasionally the school-house.

He even proffered me some land to build me a house if I would stay, preach and teach school; but my mind was bent on returning to Nauvoo.

But one evening, when I had been preaching my intended farewell sermon in the closely-packed school-house, and just at its close, a person arose and said that, God willing, he would deliver a discourse there the next Sunday, and expose the "Mormon" delusion, giving his announcement all the · force and emphasis possible.

My friends gathered at my place of stopping, and, joining with my host, prevailed upon me to stay. The word was given out that I had gone to Nauvoo.

At the time appointed a great crowd had convened—time, early candle-light.

I arrived late, purposely. My friend and I took seats near � door.

The preacher, after preliminaries, opened the Bible, and, for his text, read the 13th and 14th verses of the 16th chapter of Revelations.

After dilating upon the swampy nature of the soil contiguous to Nauvoo, styling it a good place for frogs, and facetiously comparing it to the "mouth of the dragon," he came down heavily on the "false prophet," the miracles, etc. It was a most scathing rebuke on "Mormonism."

His final peroration was on the habits of the frogs, which, while no footsteps were heard, croaked and croaked, but at the first sound of an approaching footstep, dodged their heads beneath the water. "So," said he, at the same time rising to the sublime hight of his oratory, "where, oh where is the frog that croaked here a day or two ago? Gone to that slough of iniquity, Nauvoo, the seat of the dragon and the false prophet. Why has he fled? Because he heard the footsteps of your true shepherd." After much interlarding, he dismissed by prayer.

I immediately arose and said that the frog was there yet, and would croak once more, naming the time.

Shouts from the audience named that same evening as the time, and the reverend preacher, amid jeers, cheers and cries of, "Give the boy a chance!" made for the one door.

My friend was alive to the emergency, and I, nothing loth, opened a fusilade from I. Timothy, 4th chapter, while the preacher was hemmed in by the crowd, and my friend with his back to the door.

After an exhaustive testimony of the work, we all departed, some pleased, some chagrined.

In both of the instances here narrated, the opening of the Bible to the apt and confirmatory passages, were then to my mind clearly the answer to prayer; for if ever previously read they had escaped my memory.

How much good I did on that mission, I cannot guess. One thing I do know, as a general rule not many are truly converted by the clamor of crowds, or the frenzy of debates.

My object in giving these two instances is to incite my young brethren to a study of the scriptures, the necessity of earnest secret prayer, and confidence in the promise that at the hour and time God will help them, and bring them off victoriously.

Great care must be taken to give God the glory in your after prayer, "for no flesh can glory in his sight."

Enconiums should produce humility, lest we be puffed up, and, in an after time, display our complete nothingness.

EARLY EXPERIENCE OF A LATTER-DAY SAINT,

HEAR THE GOSPEL BY CHANCE—COMPUNCTION AT SPEAKING LIGHTLY OF THE PROPHET—JOIN THE CHURCH—A NEW SUIT OF CLOTHES—OPPOSED BY RELATIVES—MY OLD FRIEND, THE BIBLE—A DREAM—REQUIRED TO RENOUNCE "MORMONISM" OR LEAVE THE HOUSE—MY RELATIVES REFUSE TO SPEAK TO ME—THEY PAWN MY CLOTHES— I RECOVER THEM—VIOLENCE USED—MY CLOTHES TORN —MY MOTHER'S DEATH—MY BROTHERS QUARREL AND CALL UPON ME TO SETTLE THEIR DIFFICULTIES—MY BROTHER SICK—HEALED IN ANSWER TO MY PRAYER.

THE substance of the following little sketch was told to the writer by the subject of it, who is an Elder in the Church, and lives in Salt Lake City. His name is Robert P——k. We give it in words as near his own as we can remember.

I was born and reared in the city of Glasgow, Scotland. I passed my boyhood without thinking much on religious matters, till I was about eighteen years of age. At this period of my life I was walking along what is called the Green, a kind of public park, when my attention was attracted by some men discussing publicly the principles of religion. One of them was a Baptist, and I could see that he had the best of

the argument, baptism by immersion being a Bible doctrine.
This was on Sunday evening.

After listening to the discussion for some time, I was
attracted to a place where another man was preaching. This
one proved to be an Elder of the Church of Jesus Christ of
Latter-day Saints.

I was so struck with the principles he advanced, that I
drank down greedily every word he spoke, and on hearing him
tell where the meeting-house of the Latter-day Saints was
situated, I went there. I was, however, too bashful to go
inside, but I walked back and forth around the building,
listening and catching whatever words I could.

I was out later than usual that night, and when I got home
I was questioned as to the cause of my absence, by my mother
(my father had been dead many years) and brothers. I said
I had been to hear the "Mormons."

"Who are the Mormons?"

"Why, the followers of Joe Smith," said I. But I had no
sooner said this than a sharp pang shot through me, and I
felt condemned for speaking thus irreverently of the prophet.
I did it because I thought it would excuse me in the eyes of
my relatives. I knew I had done wrong, for, young as I was, I
felt deeply impressed with the idea that Joseph Smith was
a prophet of God. As it was, I was severely reprimanded
for staying out so late.

Shortly after this I went to meeting and heard Elder John
Taylor speak on the setting up of the kingdom of God in the
latter days, which did a great deal towards convincing me that
the Lord had revealed the gospel in this age. After attending meeting for some time, I was finally baptized into the
Church, and was filled with joy because I knew that I was
indeed a member of the true Church of Christ.

Knowing that if my mother and four brothers discovered
that I had joined the Church I would have no peace at home,
I kept the matter secret from them. I was but an apprentice
and only earning the small sum of three shillings a week
(equal to seventy-five cents) and was, therefore, somewhat
dependent on my relatives.

I was about to get my wages raised a shilling a week, and my eldest brother, Hugh, proposed that he should get me a suit of clothes, and I pay this shilling a week until the suit was paid for, so that I might go to church with the rest of the family.

I was glad to exchange, on Sundays, my old, patched, shabby working suit for some respectable clothing, and it was agreed to.

On the following Sunday morning I went to meeting as usual, and was complimented by the President of the Branch on my improved personal appearance. When I got home in the evening the first question asked of me was,

"Where have you been?"

"I have been to meeting."

"What meeting?"

"I have been to hear the Latter-day Saints."

At this there was a perfect storm about my ears. I went and got the old family Bible, and laid down the "law and the testimony."

In answer to all they would say, I quoted and read from the Bible. I explained the principles of the gospel of Jesus, and the strongest argument any of them used was in each picking up his hat and walking out.

On the following day (Monday) I felt somewhat timid about going home in the evening, for I had dreamed on the Sunday night that my brothers were plotting to turn me out of the house.

However, home I went, and just as I approached the door I heard their voices in conversation, and they were saying they would ask me which I would choose, to leave "Mormonism" or the house; and John, who was always more rabid and unkind than the rest, said he would not even let me eat my supper until I had decided what I should do.

I walked boldly in, sat down, and commenced eating supper. They sat silent for a short time, when finally Hugh put the question to me as to whether I would renounce "Mormonism," for if I did not I would have to leave the house.

I again brought down my old friend, the family Bible, and said: "Hugh, if you will prove to me from that sacred book that I am wrong in adhering to 'Mormonism,' or rather the gospel of Christ, I will renounce it; and if I show you that you are wrong in adhering to the Church of Scotland, then you should leave that."

I then talked upon the scriptures and the principles of the gospel, and they could bring forward no reasonable objections to what I advanced.

Hugh rose to his feet and said: "If father had been alive he would have kicked you out of the house."

I answered: "Father is now rejoicing because of my having embraced the gospel of Jesus."

At this rejoinder the anger of my brothers increased, and Hugh used his old argument of picking up his hat and walking out.

I was induced to make this remark in relation to my father, because on the previous Sunday I had heard the doctrine of baptism and salvation for the dead preached by Elder John Lyon. While listening to him I was so filled with joy and gratitude at the prospect of doing something towards the salvation of my father, who had died without a knowledge of the gospel, that the tears chased each other down my face like rain. It was the first time I had heard the principles by which the grand chain which shall link the great human family together will be formed.

Seeing that threats and abuse availed nothing, making no impression upon me, my mother and brothers took another course: they would not speak to me.

Although I lived in the same house and ate at the same table with them, they uttered not a word to me, and would not answer me when I spoke to them.

Even my mother's heart seemed entirely hardened towards me, and it often cut me keenly when she would meet me on the street and pass without speaking.

Notwithstanding all this I rejoiced in the gospel exceedingly, feeling that the cause of God was more dear to me than my nearest relatives.

On the next Sunday I went to the drawer where my best suit was usually kept, and discovered that it was gone. They had not even left me a clean shirt. Nothing daunted, however, I buttoned up my shabby, old, every-day coat, and marched off to meeting, feeling that I could worship God just as fervently and acceptably in an old suit as in a new one.

Instead of handing over my wages to my mother as I usually did, I kept them every week, and announced at home my intention of doing so until my clothes were returned to me, thinking this would induce them to give them up.

However, I happened to come home one day at an unusual time, and in turning over some articles to get something I wanted, I came upon a ticket which at once explained where my clothes had gone. They had been pawned.

That this term may be understood, it may be well to say that they were deposited in a place where money is loaned on goods, and when the money is returned, with an additional sum as interest, the goods are delivered back to the owner.

I took this ticket, and with my wages which I had saved, and a little money which I had borrowed, I went to the pawn-broker's and got my clothes, and left them, for safe keeping, at the house of a brother in the Church.

I dressed up on the following Sunday and presented myself at home at dinner time, when my brothers manifested no small astonishment and a little shame on seeing that I had discovered their trick.

I had forgotten to say that on several occasions after I had dressed for meeting, my brothers would attempt to stop me from going, by main force, and several times in their efforts to keep me in, had torn the breast out of my shirt, but I invariably succeeded in getting out, and when my shirt was torn I would button up my coat and go to meeting.

Matters went on in this way for over two years, during which time I had been frequently told to leave the house and never enter it again. I paid no attention to this. On being told to go on one occasion, however, I said the next time I was ordered off I would go.

Not long afterwards my mother told me to leave the house forever, and I announced my intention of doing so on the Sunday following.

When Saturday came I proceeded to tie up my clothes in a bundle. No sooner did they see me doing this than they seized my clothing, and tore up my shirts and several other articles.

On former occasions when I had been thus abused, it was my custom to resist, but this time this disposition had departed; my heart was full; I pitied them for their blindness, and I felt like weeping tears of sorrow.

I made my way out of the house as best I could, with my wardrobe reduced to a single pair of pants, besides the clothes I wore at the time. As I was leaving I told them that the course they had taken towards me would bring them no good. My mind was filled with grief and I slept none that night.

Six weeks after this my mother burst a blood vessel, from the effect of which she never recovered, being ill from that time till her death, which occurred a year afterwards. This broke up the family.

Hugh married, and my three other brothers, John, George, and William went to live with him. Some time afterwards John came to me and told me they had quarrelled, and he wished me to go and settle matters between the brothers, which I did, and the result was that John lived apart from the others.

William, who was the most peaceable and amiable of my brothers, was taken very ill, and one evening I was impressed to go and see him. I found all the members of the family gathered around him, as he was not expected to live through the night.

After everybody had left the room but myself, he said to me, "Robert, do you believe I shall die to-night?"

I said: "No, I do not."

"I ask you because the others are hypocrites, for when I ask whether they think I will die, they say, 'No, you will live,' and then I hear them in the adjoining room arranging how they will dress me when I am dead."

He fell asleep, and I laid hands upon him and administered to him in the name of Jesus Christ, and when he awoke he was much better, and he lived for four months after this.

This is a little of my first experience as a Latter-day Saint. Nearly every true disciple of Jesus has passed through circumstances that are instructive, although trying at the time they occur, and sometimes the relating of such things has a good effect, however simple the narrative may be.

DISOBEDIENCE TO COUNSEL.

By ANSON CALL.

DRIVEN FROM MY PROPERTY BY THE MOB—DESIRE TO RETURN AND RECOVER SOME OF IT—COUNSELED BY THE CHURCH AUTHORITIES NOT TO GO—PERSIST IN GOING—VISIT A FRIENDLY FAMILY—AMIABLE INTENTION OF MY DEBTORS—MEET TWO OF THEM—THEY THREATEN MY LIFE—DESPAIR OF GETTING ANYTHING AND TRY TO START HOME—BEATEN OVER THE HEAD WITH A POLE—BARELY ESCAPE WITH MY LIFE—ASHAMED TO HAVE MY FRIENDS KNOW IT—THE LESSON I LEARNED.

TO some persons it may appear strange that the Elders of the Church in their addresses to the Saints, should so frequently dwell upon the necessity of constant obedience to counsel. But although this may seem strange, still the experience of both the Elders and the Saints goes to prove that "to obey is better than sacrifice, and to hearken than the fat of rams."

The Bible, the Book of Mormon and the Book of Doctrine and Covenants contain many instances of the blessings that have attended obedience, and the serious consequences that have followed disobedience.

I will not, however, refer to any one of these divine books; but will give my readers an instance of the consequence of disobedience which occurred to me in my early experience in the Church, in the commencement of the year 1839.

At that time I was living with the Saints in Far West, though I owned property, which I had been driven from, at the Three Forks of Grand River, distant from Far West about thirty miles.

As I wished to learn whether I could dispose of this property or not, I asked Father Joseph Smith and President Brigham Young for counsel about visiting Grand River for this purpose. They counselled me not to go; but to stay at home.

I had been driven from my property by the mob that came against the Saints, and as the Saints were obliged to leave the State I desired to go with them to Illinois. But I did not want to be burdensome to others. If I could sell my property on Grand River I would not be, so I concluded that there could not be much harm in my going to Grand River, and I set out.

How I succeeded the following extract from my journal will show.

December 31, 1838, being anxious to obtain means to make a team, that I might be able to go with the Saints, I this morning mounted the only horse I had left, and started for the Three Forks of Grand River.

I arrived at my farm on new year's day, and learned that a man by the name of George Washington O'Niel had it in his possession.

I passed on two miles further to a family by the name of Day, who had come in from the Eastern States a few weeks before I was driven away. This family had taken no part with the mob. I found the lady at home, and received from her a history of my property. She informed me that O'Niel and Culp, Missouri mobbers, had said that if ever I came to the place they would kill me; and that one Henderson and others would help them.

When on my farm I had sold store goods to a number of the citizens, who were to pay me for them at Christmas. She said she had heard many of them say that if I came there, they would pay me just as "Mormons" should be paid.

Just at this time O'Niel and Culp came into the house. They demanded of me my reasons for being there. I told them that I was attending to my business. They said I had no business there, and if I got away from there I would be smart.

I replied that I was a white man, that it was time enough to be afraid when I saw danger, and that I should go when I pleased.

They told me that they would as soon kill me as a dog, and that there would be no more notice taken of my death than if a dog were killed. This I very well understood.

They then told me that they supposed I had come to get my property.

I informed them I had; to which they replied that there was no property for me.

After repeated threatenings I became convinced that it was in vain to think of obtaining anything, and started for my horse, which was hitched at the yard fence about five rods from the door.

They followed me. O'Niel picked up the end of a hoop pole which Mr. Day had left there, he having been hooping a barrel. With this pole he struck me a blow upon the head, which nearly brought me to the ground. I looked around for a club with which to defend myself, but there was none in sight. He continued striking me, and would doubtless have killed me, had it not been for a very thick woolen cap on my head.

Mrs. Day threw open the door and cried murder. I ran for the house to get something, if possible, to defend myself with; but before I reached the door, he struck me repeatedly, and gave me one blow over the eye, the scar of which I carry to this day.

As soon as I got into the house I clutched the fire shovel. At that moment Mrs. Day closed the door, so that I could not get out nor O'Niel in. He and Culp then passed the window, on which Mrs. Day supposed they had started for their guns, so I mounted my horse and rode for Far West as fast as I could.

My head and face soon commenced swelling. On my way home I washed myself, and resolved not to inform any one

what had happened, as Father Smith and President Young
had both told me not to go.

I reached home about eleven o'clock at night, and went to
bed without making a light.   In the morning I arose, and
just as soon as I got out of bed, I fell upon the floor.
My wife was alarmed and screamed.   I told her what had
happened; but told her to keep the matter from my family.
Father Smith, however, soon heard of the occurrence, and
came to see me.   He hoped, he said, that the lesson would do
me good, and that he was glad that I was not quite killed.

Had I obeyed the words "do not go, but stay at home," I
should not have fallen into this trouble.   May you who read
this be wise, and in this particular, profit by my experience.

LORENZO DOW YOUNG'S
NARRATIVE.

CHAPTER I.

MY MOTHER'S PROMISE—CHASED BY WOLVES—A REMARK-
ABLE DREAM—THROWN FROM A HORSE—PROVIDEN-
TIALLY SAVED—RELIGIOUS REVIVAL—PREACHERS TRY IN
VAIN TO CONVERT ME—RIDICULED FOR NOT PLAYING
AT CARDS—READ INFIDEL WORKS—THEIR EFFECT—A
VISION.

I WAS born October 19th, 1807, in the town of Smyrna,
Chenango County, New York.

My mother was afflicted many years with consumption.   I
remember her as a fervent, praying woman.   She used, frequently, to call me to her bedside and counsel me to be a good
man, that the Lord might bless my future life.   On one occasion, she told me that if I would not neglect to pray to my

Heavenly Father, He would send a guardian angel to protect me in the dangers to which I might be exposed.

She had so trained me to trust in God, that, even in my early youth, I seemed capable of grasping, in my faith, the prophetic promise she had made. It sank deep into my heart, and ever since has been an anchor of hope in the difficulties and dangers to which I have been exposed.

This pious, faithful, friend and mother, drooped and died on the 11th of June, 1814.

Soon after her death, my father broke up housekeeping, and I was sent about sixty miles to live with my brother-in-law, John P. Green, near Cayuga Bridge.

It was a marshy, malarious country, and I was taken very sick with fever and ague, with which I suffered severely. In the fall of 1815, we removed to Tyrone, Schuyler County. In the meantime, my father had taken up some land on which to make a home, about six miles from where Mr. Green lived. This country, at that time, was new, and there was nothing but a dense forest between Mr. Green's house and my father's. The wolves were very numerous in this forest. At one time, several of them chased me to Mr. Green's house, and I seemed to barely escape with my life.

During the winter of 1815-16, in company with my brothers, Joseph, Phinehas and Brigham, I worked for my father and assisted him to clear off some land.

In the autumn of 1816, when about nine years old, I had a peculiar dream. I thought I stood in an open, clear space of ground, and saw a plain, fine road, leading, at an angle of 45° degrees, into the air, as far as I could see. I heard a noise like a carriage in rapid motion, at what seemed the upper end of the road. In a moment it came in sight. It was drawn by a pair of beautiful, white horses. The carriage and harness appeared brilliant with gold. The horses traveled with the speed of the wind. It was made manifest to me that the Savior was in the carriage, and that it was driven by His servant. The carriage stopped near me, and the Savior inquired where my brother Brigham was. After informing Him, He further inquired about my other brothers, and our father. After I had answered His inquiries, He stated that

He wanted us all, but He especially wanted my brother Brigham. The team then turned right about, and returned on the road it had come.

I awoke at once, and slept no more that night. I felt frightened, and supposed we were all going to die. I saw no other solution to the dream. It was a shadowing of our future which I was then in no condition to discern.

In the morning I told my father the dream, and my fears that we were going to die. He comforted me with the assurance that he did not think my interpretation was correct.

In the winter of 1817-18, I went to live with my brother-in-law, James Little, in the town of Aurelius, Cayuga County, New York. I remained there about five years, learning the business of a gardener and fruit raiser.

In the summer of my twelfth year, I was placed upon a race horse by Mr. Little, and sent on an errand. The animal was too spirited for a boy of my age to safely ride. It became frightened and unmanageable. It turned so rapidly around that I was thrown out of the saddle. As I fell my bare foot slipped through the iron stirrup, where I hung with my head just touching the ground. With my left hand, I still grasped the bridle rein, on that side, firmly. The horse endeavored to kick me, but, fortunately, did not succeed on account of my being too close to him. My hold on the bridle rein prevented the animal from running away and caused him to whirl around almost in a circle.

In danger we often think with great rapidity. I comprehended my situation in a moment, and, at first, could see no way of escape from having my brains dashed out. But, as I hung, I was suddenly impressed to get hold of the stirrup with my right hand, and make an effort to raise myself up, so as to get my foot loose from it. By a great effort I succeeded in drawing myself up, and slipping the stirrup over my foot. I then let go all hold and fell to the ground.

The horse went at full speed for home and his stable. I got up and was not much hurt.

The promise my mother made me flashed into my mind, and I felt thankful to the Lord that I had been preserved from serious harm by a kind providence.

In the winter of 1819-20, I left Aurelius and went about twenty miles to Hector, Schuyler County. A Methodist revival occurred in that town, and religious excitement ran so high that it became fashionable to make a profession of religion.

So far as I knew, every young person in the neighborhood but myself professed to receive "a saving change of heart" before the close of the revival.

As was usual during such periods of religious excitement, meetings were held nightly. In these meetings it was the custom to request those who were "seeking religion," to come forward to some seat reserved for the purpose, to be prayed for.

I was somewhat affected by the intense religious feeling. One evening, I attended a meeting presided over by Elder Gilmore, the leading minister. Two or three other preachers were also present. The usual invitation was given for penitents to come forward to the "anxious seat."

Some time was spent in prayer, when all who had come forward, except myself, professed to have a "change of heart." The meeting was closed, and Elder Gilmore proposed that those who were willing to do so, should retire to a private house with me, and continue in prayer till I was converted.

As proposed, we retired to a neighboring house, where the praying continued until two o'clock in the morning.

Elder Gilmore then asked me if I had not received a "change of heart."

I replied that I had not realized any "change."

After so much fruitless labor, they were evidently disposed to give me up as a reprobate. Elder Gilmore told me that I had sinned away the day of grace, and my damnation was sure. He asserted that he would never offer another prayer for me.

Although religious in my nature, even at that early age, sectarian religion seemed empty and void.

The following morning, I left the scene of this religious excitement in Hector and returned to Cayuga County, about three miles from Auburn. There I went to work for Mr. Monroe, to learn the trade of a blacksmith. He carried on considerable business, and employed a number of young men and apprentices.

One evening, Mr. Monroe and the workmen gathered around the center table, in the sitting room, to while away the evening in a game of cards. Mr. Monroe invited me to participate.

My father had counseled me never to play a game of cards. "Not," said he, "that there is any particular harm in playing a game of cards, but card-playing has a tendency to lead those who follow it into other vices."

I determined, at the time, to keep his counsel should it cost me my situation. Mr. Monroe did not appear disposed to receive any apology for not accepting his invitation. I arose, took a Bible that was near me, and read during the evening while the remainder of the company played cards.

The most of Mr. Monroe's workmen were inclined to infidelity, and the course I took that evening, afterwards brought upon me much annoyance and ridicule.

. Although infidel in principle, Mr. Monroe was kind to those around him, and manifested that kindness to me as well as others. He placed in my hands several infidel books. Among them, I recollect the writings of Voltaire and Thomas Payne. My experience at this time, taught me that skeptical works cannot be read without leaving their impression on the mind. A continuation of reading them must, eventually, lead to confirmed infidelity.

The teachings of my pious parents had given me considerable faith in God, and I enjoyed some of His Spirit. It has since been evident to me, that the reading of those infidel books stirred up an antagonism in me between the Spirit of truth and the spirit of skepticism. The struggle between them, in my bosom, continued about a year, and was a source of great affliction to me. The Lord, through His Spirit, was trying to save me from error and darkness.

I would advise all my young friends, and especially those who have had the testimony of the Spirit of truth, to never, by any act of theirs, invite the spirit of infidelity into their hearts, lest they fall away into darkness, and go down to death.

I remained with Mr. Monroe nearly two years. I injured myself lifting a log, and it was evident that I could not again work at the blacksmith business for some time. For this reason I left Mr. Monroe, and went to visit Mr. J. P. Green, who lived in Watertown, about one hundred miles from Auburn, in Jefferson County.

For sometime my health continued poor. One day I lay on a bed to rest where I could see the family in their ordinary occupations. All at once I heard the most beautiful music. I soon discovered from whence it came. Standing side by side, on the foot board of the beadstead on which I lay, were two beautiful, seraph-like beings, about the size of children seven or eight years old. They were dressed in white, and appeared surpassingly pure and heavenly. I felt certain that I was fully awake, and these juvenile personages were realistic to me. With their disappearance the music ceased. I turned and asked two of my sisters, who were in the room, if they had not heard the music. I was much surprised to learn that they had heard nothing.

CHAPTER II.

MARRIAGE—A VISION OF OTHER WORLDS—MY RELUCTANCE AT RETURNING TO A MORTAL EXISTENCE—A PROMISE WITH CONDITIONS—I EXHORT OTHERS TO FAITHFULNESS.

WHILE at Watertown, I married, and afterwards removed to Mendon, Monroe County. At this place I had a remarkable dream or vision. I fancied that I died. In a moment I was out of the body, and fully conscious that I had made the change. At once, a heavenly messenger, or guide, was by me. I thought and acted as naturally as I had done in the body, and all my sensations seemed as complete without as with it. The personage with me was dressed in the purest white. For a short time I remained in the room where my body lay. My sister Fanny (who was living with me when I had this dream) and my wife were weeping bitterly over my death. I sympathized with them deeply in their sorrow, and desired to comfort them. I realized that I was under the control of the man who was by me. I begged of him the privilege of speaking to them, but he said he could not grant it. My guide, for so I will call him, said "Now let us go."

Space seemed annihilated. Apparently we went up, and almost instantly were in another world. It was of such magnitude that I formed no conception of its size. It was filled with innumerable hosts of beings, who seemed as naturally human as those among whom I had lived. With some I had been acquainted in the world I had just left. My guide informed me that those I saw had not yet arrived at their final abiding place. All kinds of people seemed mixed up promiscuously, as they are in this world. Their surroundings and manner indicated that they were in a state of expectation, and awaiting some event of considerable moment to them.

As we went on from this place, my guide said, "I will now show you the condition of the damned." Pointing with his hand, he said, "Look!"

I looked down a distance which appeared incomprehensible to me. I gazed on a vast region filled with multitudes of beings. I could see everything with the most minute distinctness. The multitude of people I saw were miserable in the extreme. "These," said my guide, "are they who have rejected the means of salvation, that were placed within their reach, and have brought upon themselves the condemnation you behold."

The expression of the countenances of these sufferers was clear and distinct. They indicated extreme remorse, sorrow and dejection. They appeared conscious that none but themselves were to blame for their forlorn condition.

This scene affected me much, and I could not refrain from weeping.

Again my guide said, "Now let us go."

In a moment we were at the gate of a beautiful city. A porter opened it and we passed in. The city was grand and beautiful beyond anything that I can describe. It was clothed in the purest light, brilliant but not glaring or unpleasant.

The people, men and women, in their employments and surroundings, seemed contented and happy. I knew those I met without being told who they were. Jesus and the ancient apostles were there. I saw and spoke with the apostle Paul.

My guide would not permit me to pause much by the way, but rather hurried me on through this place to another still higher but connected with it. It was still more beautiful and glorious than anything I had before seen. To me its extent and magnificence were incomprehensible.

My guide pointed to a mansion which excelled everything else in perfection and beauty. It was clothed with fire and intense light. It appeared a fountain of light, throwing brilliant scintillations of glory all around it, and I could conceive of no limit to which these emanations extended. Said my guide, "That is where God resides." He permitted me to enter this glorious city but a short distance. Without speaking, he motioned that we would retrace our steps.

We were soon in the adjoining city. There I met my mother, and a sister who died when six or seven years old. These I knew at sight without an introduction.

After mingling with the pure and happy beings of this place a short time, my guide said again, "Let us go."

We were soon through the gate by which we had entered the city. My guide then said, "Now we will return."

I could distinctly see the world from which we had first come. It appeared to be a vast distance below us. To me, it looked cloudy, dreary and dark. I was filled with sad disappointment, I might say horror, at the idea of returning there. I supposed I had come to stay in that heavenly place, which I had so long desired to see; up to this time, the thought had not occurred to me that I would be required to return.

I plead with my guide to let me remain. He replied that I was permitted to only visit these heavenly cities, for I had not filled my mission in yonder world; therefore I must return and take my body. If I was faithful to the grace of God which would be imparted to me, if I would bear a faithful testimony to the inhabitants of the earth of a sacrificed and risen Savior, and His atonement for man, in a little time I should be permitted to return and remain.

These words gave me comfort and inspired my bosom with the principle of faith. To me, these things were real. I felt that a great mission had been given me, and I accepted it in my heart. The responsibility of that mission has rested on me from that time until now.

We returned to my house. There I found my body, and it appeared to me dressed for burial. It was with great reluctance that I took possession of it to resume the ordinary avocations of life, and endeavor to fill the important mission I had received. I awoke and found myself in my bed. I lay and meditated the remainder of the night on what had been shown me.

Call it a dream, or vision, or what I may, what I saw was as real to every sense of my being as anything I have passed through. The memory of it is clear and distinct with me to-day, after the lapse of fifty years with its many changes.

From that time, although belonging to no church, the Spirit was with me to testify to the sufferings and atonement of the Savior. As I had opportunity, I continually exhorted the people, in public and private, to exercise faith in the Lord Jesus Christ, to repent of their sins and live a life of righteousness and good works.

CHAPTER III.

I TAKE TO PREACHING—MAKE MANY CONVERTS—REFUSE
TO BAPTIZE THEM—THEY ARE BAPTIZED BY A CAMP-
BELLITE PREACHER—·URGED TO JOIN THE CAMPBELLITES
—REFUSE, AND THE DEVIL TEMPTS ME—I GRIEVE THE
SPIRIT, BUT REGAIN IT THROUGH FASTING AND PRAYER
—HEAR THE GOSPFL—VISIT FROM ELDER GIFFORD—HE
IS THREATENED WITH TAR AND FEATHERS—MY BROTHER
AND I DEFEND HIM.

IN the fall of 1828, I returned to Hector, Schuyler County, New
York. Quite a number of people lived there of the Campbellite faith. 'Squire Chase, a prominent man in the neighborhood, who had been a preacher of the sect, said that they
were cold in religion and had not held any meetings for several
months. I had been there but a few days, when I went with
him about two miles to a Methodist meeting. This occurred
in the month of November.

Up to this time I had joined no church, although I had
professed religion, attended meetings, and preached when I
had an opportunity.

On my return, I remarked to Mr. Chase, "Why cannot we
have meetings in our neighborhood as well as to go so far to
them?"

·He replied, "We are all dead there; we would have meetings but I do not feel like preaching. But if you will do the
preaching, I will appoint a meeting."

He did so. The first two meetings but few attended. The
third meeting the house was crowded. Finally, meetings
were held nearly every night in the week, and were well
attended. A reformation started among the people, and
there were quite a number of religious converts. Campbellite
principles had long prevailed in the neighborhood. The converts desired baptism, as that was a prominent principle in
the Campbellite faith. Mr. Chase urged me to perform the

ordinance. I excused myself by telling him that I had never joined any religious denomination, and did not feel authorized to administer it. I finally utterly refused to do so. He then sent forty or fifty miles for Elder Brown, a regular Campbellite preacher.

He came and baptized about sixty converts and organized a branch of the Campbellite church out of the fruits of my labors. He quite exhausted his persuasive powers to induce me to join the Campbellite church, to take a circuit and go to preaching.

I told him I would not preach his doctrines. If I preached at all, I should preach the whole Bible as I understood it.

He said I could do so, for he did not think I would preach anything wrong.

A spirit worked with me to do all the good I could, but not to join any religious denomination. It prevailed within me against all temptation this time. Perhaps the guardian angel, promised by my mother, watched over my spiritual as well as temporal welfare.

I think, at the time of this reformation, I had as much of the Spirit of the Lord with me as I could well enjoy in my ignorance of the gospel in its purity. I was full of the testimony of the truth as I understood it.

This reformation in Hector, was a means of temptation to me. I had preached and labored with my might to lead the people to the truth, and Elder Brown had stepped in and reaped the results of my labors. Because I would not join the Campbellite church and preach for them, I was entirely thrown aside. The adversary would reason with me thus: "What is the use of all your preaching? It does not amount to anything to you. You had better attend to your own business and let such nonsense alone."

I listened to these suggestions until I had grieved the Spirit of the Lord which I had enjoyed. I no longer had the Spirit to pray or to exhort the people to lives of righteousness. I was in this condition for several months.

In all this lethargy and darkness, I knew there was such a thing as joy in the Spirit of God—that in the testimony of Jesus there was light and peace. I knew I had accepted a mission to bear this testimony while I should remain on the earth.

Knowing these things, I became, in time, alarmed at my conditon, I feared that the Lord had forsaken me. I humbled myself before Him in fasting and prayer. I promised Him that if He would return His good Spirit, I would never again reject its suggestions.

Matters continued thus with me for several weeks. In one of my seasons of prayer and supplication, I sensibly felt that I was again visited by the Holy Spirit. I was encouraged to resume my labors in exhorting the people whenever an opportunity was presented. I went from home on the Sabbath and held meetings in different places. I was employed in this way when I first saw the Book of Mormon, and when the gospel was preached to me.

This, and other experiences, have convinced me that when we question the Holy Spirit it is likely to be grieved, and leave us to ourselves. Then will our darkness be greater than if we had never enjoyed its influences. Perhaps this incident in my life may suggest wisdom to others.

In November, 1829, I removed to a place called Hector Hill. In February, 1831, my father, my brothers Joseph and Brigham, and Heber C. Kimball came to my house. They brought with them the Book of Mormon. They were on their way to visit some Saints in Pennsylvania. Through fear of being deceived, I was quite cautious in religious matters. I read and compared the Book of Mormon with the Bible, and fasted and prayed that I might come to a knowledge of the truth. The Spirit seemed to say, "This is the way; walk ye in it." This was all the testimony I could get at the time; it was not altogether satisfactory.

The following May, Elder Levi Gifford came into the neighborhood, and desired to preach. My brother, John, belonged to the Methodist church, and had charge of their meeting house which was in the neighborhood. I obtained from him permission for Elder Gifford to preach in it. The appointment was circulated for a meeting the same evening.

This was on Saturday evening, and the circuit preacher of that district was to hold a meeting there on Sunday.

Elder Midbury, the circuit preacher, attended the meeting. The house was crowded. As soon as Elder Gifford had concluded his discourse, Elder Midbury arose to his feet and said: "Brethren, sisters and friends: I have been a preacher of the gospel for twenty-two years; I do not know that I have been the means of converting a sinner, or reclaiming a poor backslider; but this I do know, that the doctrine the stranger has preached to us to-night is a deception, that Joe Smith is a false prophet, and that the Book of Mormon is from hell."

After talking awhile in this strain, he concluded. I immediately arose to my feet and asked the privilege of speaking, which was granted. I said that Elder Midbury, in his remarks, entirely ignored the possibility of more revelation, and acknowledged that he had been a preacher of the gospel for twenty-two years, without knowing that he had been the means of converting a sinner, or of reclaiming a poor backslider. But still he claimed to know that the doctrine he had just heard was false, that Joseph Smith was an impostor, and that the Book of Mormon was from hell. "Now, how is it possible," I asked, "for him to know these things unless he has received a revelation?"

When I sat down a strong man, by the name of Thompson, who was well known in the neighborhood as a beligerent character, stepped up to Elder Gifford and demanded the proofs of the authenticity of the Book of Mormon.

Elder Gifford replied, "I have said all I care about saying to-night."

Then said Mr. Thompson, "we will take the privilege of clothing you with a coat of tar and feathers, and riding you out of town on a rail."

In the meantime, four or five others of like character came to the front.

Acting under the impulse of the moment—true to the instincts of my nature to protect the weak against the strong, I stepped between Elder Gifford and Mr. Thompson. Looking the latter in the eye, I said, "Mr. Thompson, you cannot lay your hand on this stranger to harm a hair of his head, without you do it over my dead body."

He replied by mere threats of violence, which brought my brother John to his feet.

With a voice and manner, that carried with it a power greater than I had ever seen manifested in him before, and, I might say, since, he commanded Mr. Thompson and party to take their seats. He continued, "Gentlemen, if you offer to lay a hand on Mr. Gifford, you shall pass through my hands, after which I think you will not want any more to-night." Mr. Thompson and party quieted down and then took their seats.

Since then the Elders have passed through so many similar experiences, that they have ceased to be a novelty. That there should be such a powerful antagonism of spirits manifesting themselves in muscle, in a Christian church, indicated a new era in religious influences.

CHAPTER IV.

CONVERTED — START FOR MISSOURI — CALLED TO PREACH "MORMONISM" WITHOUT BEING BAPTIZED — JOIN THE CHURCH—VOYAGE TO PITTSBURG —PREACH THE GOSPEL AND ESTABLISH A BRANCH—EXPERIENCE AS A TRUNK-MAKER—— MISSION TO NEW YORK—SPEAK IN TONGUES EFFECTS OF PREACHING COUNTERACTED BY LIES—SECOND VOYAGE DOWN THE OHIO—PROVIDENTIAL DELAY.

IN the spring of 1831 there was a two-days meeting of the Saints, about six miles from where I lived, in the State of Pennsylvania. I attended it, and became fully convinced of the divine origin of the latter-day work.

In the summer of 1831, I settled up my business and started for the latter-day Zion, in the State of Missouri. On my way out of the State of New York, I visited Elder J. P. Green, in the town of Avon.

As I arrived there on Saturday, he said, "Brother Lorenzo, I am very glad you have come. I have an appointment to preach at 10 o'clock, eight miles from here, but I am very unwell and not able to fill it. I want you to do it for me."

I rather ridiculed the idea, saying, "You want me to preach as a Mormon Elder, when I have not even joined the Church?" He still desired me to go, and said, "it will be all right."

E. M. Green, the son of J. P. Green, accompanied me, with a revelation on the organization of the Chuch, which his father directed him to read to the congregation.

Arriving at the place appointed, I found the house full, and a Baptist preacher in the stand. I introduced myself to the minister; he invited the congregation to sing, and I prayed, and E. M. Green read the revelation. I arose and commenced to speak. The good Spirit was with me, and I had much freedom. I talked about one hour and a quarter. At the close I gave any one the privilege of speaking who wished to. The Baptist minister arose and bore his testimony, that what they had heard was true Bible doctrine, and could not be questioned.

After meeting, several persons gathered around me and wished to be baptized. Knowing that I had not received authority to administer the ordinance, I put them off, telling them that when Elder Green came to fill the next appointment that had been made for him, he would baptize them. Among those who requested baptism, at that time, were the brothers Joseph and Chandler Holbrook, and Mary Ann Angell, now the relict of President Brigham Young.

On the following morning I told Elder Green that, inasmuch as I had believed in the gospel for some time, and had preached as a "Mormon" Elder, I thought it was time that I was baptized. He administered the ordinance, and ordained me an Elder. I then went on my way rejoicing.

In due time I reached Olean Point, on the Alleghany river, one of the streams that form the head waters of the Ohio. Several families had gathered there with the view of descending the river in boats. Among them were my brother Phineas and his family. The company built two boats, and started down the Alleghany river, in the month of November.

The river was low and falling. It was my lot, with others, nearly every morning to get into the water and work the boats off the sand bars upon which we anchored at night. The water was always cold, and at times the ice was half an inch thick. I had the whooping cough, and this work was very severe on me.

We journeyed in this way for three weeks, to Pittsburg, at the head of the Ohio river. Three days before arriving there my wife was taken sick, and did not feel that she could travel any farther.

Brother Phineas and I concluded to stop awhile in Pittsburg. We were destitute of money, having only fifty cents left between us. Soon after tying up our boat, a report got noised about that we were a party of "Mormons," on our way to Zion. Some of the ideas of the Saints in regard to gathering, although often stated erroneously, had obtained quite an extensive circulation in the country. Many of the people came to see us, and at first, stared as though beholding some great curiosity. My brother Phineas and I hired one room and moved into it. We retained one boat and the remainder of the company went on in the other.

The way we traveled would now be thought a novel and hard way for the Saints to gather in these days of railroads. Fifty years have made many changes, The world is progressing.

Some respectable-looking men inquired if there were any "Mormon" preachers in the company. We informed them that we were Elders. They expressed a wish that we would hold a meeting.

We soon learned that Mr. Wm. Harris, of whom we had rented our room, had somewhere met one of our Elders, learned something of the gospel, and had been baptized. Up to that time he had made no open profession of having joined the Saints.

There was a large room in the same house we had moved into. This Brother Harris offered us for holding meetings in. The first evening quite a goodly number gathered into it, and my brother Phineas and I talked to them. Before closing, we gave the privilege for any one to speak who wished to.

An elderly lady arose and said she had been seeking for the truth many years, and that she had read the Bible through from Genesis to Revelations fourteen times, with a prayerful heart, that she might come to a knowledge of the truth. She testified that what she had just heard was the first gospel discourse she had ever heard in her life. Almost in the words of the eunuch to Phillip, she said: "Here is water, what hinders me from being baptized?"

The house stood on the bank of the Alleghany river. The night was dark, and we thought it dangerous to try to baptize her.

She called to our minds the case of the jailor, who was baptized in the self-same hour in which he believed.

We obtained a lantern and went to the bank of the river, the people following us. We found the bank steep and the water somewhat deep; but my brother, Phineas, held on to me while I baptized the woman.

We continued to hold meetings and baptize until over thirty persons had united with the Church.

We had authority to preach, baptize and confirm, but we had no knowledge of the organization of the Church, and knew not how to organize a branch. In the following winter, of 1831-32, Elder Sidney Rigdon passed through Pittsburg, and gave us instructions concerning the organization of the Church. We then organized a branch, and continued our meetings.

After events have passed, we often see in them a providence leading to important results. We left our homes in the State of New York for Missouri, the only objective point in which we felt any interest. A seeming chance of sickness induced us to stop for a season in Pittsburg. There we found a people ready to receive the truth. We preached the gospel, and built up a branch of the Church. We were evidently led there for the accomplishment of this important work.

As will be seen, we subsequently went to Kirtland, instead of going on west. But before going to Kirtland, there was yet another place where we were to preach the gospel.

As before stated, on our arrival in Pittsburg our finances were low. Brother Phineas soon obtained labor. I was not so successful, I walked the streets of the town day after day, in search of a job, willing to accept of anything I could possibly do. Finally I met a man who gave me some encouragement. Said he, "Are you a mechanic?"

I felt constrained to answer "yes," although I could not really lay much claim to the profession.

"Well, said he, I want twelve dozen steamboat trunks made." I replied, "I am your man, but I am traveling. I have stopped here on account of sickness in my family, and have no tools with me, and no place to work. He assured me that he had shop, tools and everything necessary to work with. We went at once to his shop.

I really did not know what a steamboat trunk was. I told him that I was from the Eastern States, where probably they worked different to what they did in that country, and I should feel much obliged if he would lay out a trunk for me, that I might make no mistake. He picked up a wide board, laid it on a bench, and with square and compass soon laid out a trunk. "There," said he, "that is the way I do it; but if it don't suit you, do it as you have a mind to," and he walked out of the shop. Food and comforts for my family were at stake. I knelt down and asked the Lord to enable me to do the work in an acceptable manner, and I arose and went to work with a light heart. I got the bodies of several trunks together that day. Towards evening my employer came in, examined my work carefully, and said, "That is good enough. If you will do them all as well as that, it will do." I put together the twelve dozen trunks, covered and finished them off to my employer's satisfaction, and he paid me the money.

For that kindly providence I felt thankful. From that time I found labor and soon made my family quite comfortable.

In the spring of 1832, it was thought best that I should go on a mission to the State of New York. I spent the summer in preaching the gospel. I had joy in my labors, being instrumental in bringing many into the Church.

I visited the town of Hector, where, by my preaching, as before stated, a Campbellite church had been organized. I preached in the same house that I had occupied on the previous occasion. Soon after I commenced to talk, such a spirit of darkness and opposition prevailed in the house, that for the first and only time in my life, I was entirely bound. I stood speechless. The congregation looked at me as if wondering what could be the matter. A sensation such as I had never felt before came over me. My tongue seemed numb or paralyzed. In a short time I commenced to speak in an unknown tongue. I probably spoke about fifteen minutes. Soon after ceasing to talk, the interpretation came clear and distinct to my mind. I at once gave it to the congregation.

I had no further difficulty. I talked about an hour. My old friend, Squire Chase, arose and testified that what he had heard was the truth, and that the power of God had been made manifest. He and several others shed tears. Their hearts were softened by the influence of the good Spirit.

I had some prior engagements to meet at a considerable distance from Hector. These would keep me away about two weeks. I regretted the necessity of going away, and left an appointment for another meeting on my return. I indulged in the hope of establishing a branch of the Church there.

While I was absent, the Elder Brown, who had organized a Campbellite Church from converts made by my preaching, heard that I was preaching "Mormonism." He came there, held meetings and visited from house to house. He repeated to the people all the extravagant stories and falsehoods about the Prophet Joseph and the Book of Mormon, which were so extensively circulated in those early times. When I returned, I found the minds of the people filled with prejudice and bitterness. The Spirit manifested to me that more preaching to them would be in vain, and I went away sorrowing. I have not heard since that any of that people have ever joined the Church.

I went to Avon, Genesee County, to see my father, John Young. He desired to go west and see the Prophet. His wife, my stepmother, preferred to remain with her children.

He had previously sold out his property in the town of Mendon for several hundred dollars, and had used it to supply the wants of the Elders. He had served as a soldier during three campaigns of the revolutionary war. About this time, he received a penison from the government. This furnished him the means of accompanying me to Pittsburg. On arriving there, my brother Phineas and I bought a family boat, in which we went twenty-five miles down the Ohio River. My wife was again so sick that we felt compelled to stop at Beardstown.

The people came to see us, and soon learned that we were "Mormons." They expressed a wish that we would preach to them. The following day being Sunday, we consented to do so if they would furnish a house. Mr. Isaac Hill, since Bishop for several years of the 2nd Ward of Salt Lake City, was then a citizen of that place. Through his kindly offices the school house was opened for us.

After the first meeting, the people desired more. In a few days we baptized five persons, among them Mr. Hill and Peter Shirts. The latter is well known to many of the people of Utah.

In a short time, my brother Phineas went to Kirtland with our father. The Saints desired that I should remain at Beardstown, and I concluded to spend the winter there. Some of my friends, thinking that I might get work easier at West Union, five miles from Beardstown, I removed there. There, although my way at first seemed hedged up, I succeeded in making my family comfortable through the winter. Again we had been providentially directed to where there were a few ready to receive the truth.

CHAPTER V.

REMOVAL TO KIRTLAND—WORK UPON THE TEMPLE—A LES-
SON—SICKNESS—PRONOUNCED INCURABLE BY DOCTORS
—HEALED IN ANSWER TO PRAYER—CURED OF LAME-
NESS — REMOVAL TO MISSOURI — COMMENCEMENT OF
HOSTILITIES—SURROUNDED BY A MOB—FACE DEATH—
RESCUED.

IN March, 1833, I removed to Kirtland. The Kirtland Temple committee was appointed June 6th, 1833. About that time, I took with my team Brothers Hyrum and Joseph Smith, Reynolds Cahoon and my brother Brigham, to look at a stone quarry, and see if the rock was suitable for the walls of the temple. It was decided that it would do, and a part of a load was put on the wagon. We all returned to town, and the rock was unloaded on the temple ground. As near as I recollect, this was the first rock hauled for that building.

From that time I worked with the brethren, as occasion required, until the temple was completed. On the 17th of February, 1834, those holding the Priesthood were called together to organize a High Council. I was one of the number. On that occasion I committed a great error. That it may be a lesson for others, is my reason for relating it here. The Prophet requested me to take a seat with other brethren who had been selected for this Council.

Instead of doing as requested, I arose and plead my inability to fill so responsible a position, manifesting, I think, considerable earnestness in the matter. The Prophet then said that he really desired that I should take the place.

Still excusing myself, he appointed another to fill it. I think this was the reason the Prophet never again called me to fill any important position in the Priesthood during his life.

I have since learned to go where I am called, and not set up my judgment against that of those who are called to lead in this kingdom.

When the temple was enclosed, in a meeting of the brethren, called to consult about its completion, the Prophet desired that a hard finish be put on its outside walls. None of the masons who had worked on the building knew how to do it. Looking around on the brethren, his eyes rested upon me; he said, "Brother Lorenzo. I want you to take hold and get this finish on the walls. Will you do it?"

"Yes;" I replied; "I will try." The following day, with horse and buggy I went to Cleveland, twenty-two miles, determined, if possible, to find a man who understood the business of putting a hard finish on the walls. I had been there but a short time, inquiring after such a man, when I met a young man who said he understood the business, had just completed a job, and wanted another. I employed him at once, put him and his tools into the buggy, and returned to Kirtland.

We soon had the materials and fixtures on hand to make the mortar. In a short time the finish was being put upon the walls.

I made a suitable tool and, before the mortar was dry, I marked off the walls into blocks in imitation of regular stone work. When the finish was on I commenced penciling.

It was then the last of November, and the weather daily grew colder. A Brother Stillman assisted me a day or two, but said that he could not stand the cold, and quit the work.

I continued, day after day, determined, if possible, to complete the job. When I got badly chilled I went into my house, warmed myself and returned again to the work.

I completed the task in the fore part of December, but was sick the last two days. I had caught a bad cold, had a very severe cough, and, in a few days was confined to my bed.

My disease was pronouned to be the quick consumption. I sank rapidly for six or seven weeks. For two weeks I was unable to talk. Dr. Williams, one of the brethren, came to see me, and, considering my case a bad one, came the next day and brought with him Dr. Seely, an old practicing physician, and another doctor whose name I have forgotten.

They passed me through an examination. Dr. Seely asserted
that I had not as much lungs left as would fill a tea saucer.
He appeared a somewhat rough, irreligious man. Probably,
with what he considered a good-natured fling at our belief in
miracles, he said to my father, as he left the house:

"Mr. Young, unless the Lord makes your son a new pair
of lungs, there is no hope for him!"

At this time I was so low and nervous that I could scarcely
bear any noise in the room. The next morning after the
visit of the doctors, my father came to the door of the room
to see how I was. I recollect his gazing earnestly at me with
tears in his eyes. As I afterwards learned, he went from
there to the Prophet Joseph, and said to him: "My son
Lorenzo is dying; can there not be something done for him?"

The Prophet studied a little while, and replied, "Yes! Of
necessity, I must go away to fill an appointment, which I cannot put off. But you go and get my brother Hyrum, and,
with him, get together twelve or fifteen good faithful brethren; go to the house of Brother Lorenzo, and all join in
prayer. One be mouth and the others repeat after him in
unison. After prayer, divide into quorums of three. Let the
first quorum who administer, anoint Brother Young with oil;
then lay hands on him, one being mouth and the other two
repeating in unison after him. When all the quorums have,
in succession, laid their hands on Brother Young and prayed for
him, begin again with the first quorum, by anointing with oil
as before, continuing the administration in this way until
you receive a testimony that he will be restored."

My father came with the brethren, and these instructions
were strictly followed. The administrations were continued
until it came the turn of the first quorum the third time.
Brother Hyrum Smith led. The Spirit rested mightily upon
him. He was full of blessing and prophecy. Among other
things, he said that I should live to go with the Saints into
the bosom of the Rocky Mountains, to build up a place there,
and that my cellar should overflow with wine and fatness.

At that time, I had not heard about the Saints going to
the Rocky Mountains; possibly Brother Smith had. After
he had finished he seemed surprised at some things he had

said, and wondered at the manifestations of the Spirit. I coughed no more after that administration, and rapidly recovered.

I had been pronounced by the best physicians in the country past all human aid, and I am a living witness of the power of God manifested in my behalf through the administration of the Elders.

I continued to live in Kirtland, labored for the support of my family and went on missions until September, 1837. At that time there was considerable persecution, and many Saints left for Missouri. In company with Brother Isaac Decker and family, I started for that place.

On account of sickness in my family, I laid by at Dublin, Indiana. I remained there until January, 1838.

I went to Cincinnati. While absent, my brother Brigham, and Brothers Joseph and Samuel Smith, with their families, came along on their way to Missouri. They were accompanied by Brother Daniel Holman and Brother Miles. I returned to Dublin, and, in February, we continued our journey together.

On the way, in jumping from a wagon, I fell and split my knee pan on a sharp stone. The injury was both painful and dangerous. .

Riding over rough roads in a loaded wagon was very painful to me. At Terre Haute, Indiana, my leg was examined by a surgeon. He said even if I got well, my leg would always be stiff. However, my faith was that I should again have the use of it. It was still over four hundred miles to our destination. I suffered much, but got the use of my leg the following summer. I attribute this result to the blessing of the Lord through the administration of the Elders.

On our way, we crossed the Mississippi river at Quincy, Illinois, on the ice. We were the last to cross in that way that season. When near the west side, on account of the weakness of the ice, we took the horses from the wagons and laid down planks to run the latter to the shore.

In March, Brother Isaac Decker and I arrived in Davis County, Missouri. I purchased a quarter section of land and went to work to make me a home. Brother Decker rented a farm. The remainder of the company went on to Far West, twenty-two miles farther.

We labored diligently at our business during the summer, usually having meetings on the Sabbath. Matters remained quiet until election day, August 6th, 1838, when the Missourians determined that the "Mormons" should not vote. On the other hand, the brethren asserted their rights, and a fight took place at Gallatin, as related in Church history. I did not feel like attending election, and did not go. This was the beginning of our troubles in Davis County.

I lived eighteen miles from Adam Ondi-Ahman. About this time, I left my family on my place and went there and stood guard some two weeks. Brother Decker accompanied me. After completing our term of military service, Brother Decker and I started for home. We had but one horse, and we alternately rode and walked. As we passed through the town of Gallatin, about eight miles from home, it was my turn to walk, and Brother Decker was ahead of me on the horse. There was a company of Missourians stationed about twenty rods from the road, near a whisky saloon. As I was passing nearly opposite them, a party of men stepped in front of me and the leader ordered me to stop. He was armed with a sword. There were twenty-two of the party, mostly armed with rifles.

Nothing was said to Brother Decker, although he halted and sat on his horse a short distance off and watched the proceedings.

The captain of the party asked me where I had been, where I was going, and if I was a "Mormon," with many other questions which I answered truthfully.

After answering one of his questions, with a profane epithet he called me a liar. After this, I kept my mouth closed and answered no more of his questions. He was about half drunk, as were probably some of his men. He became much irritated at my silence, and used very profane and abusive language. Said he: "You have probably been robbing and burning in this section, and ought to be killed. Anyhow, I will make you open your mouth." He then ordered his men to form in a half circle a little distance from

me, evidently to concentrate their fire.   He then ordered
them to "Make ready! Aim!"

Every rifle was drawn on me. I prayed in my heart, and
felt considerable assurance that they would not be permitted
to kill me. My life trembled in the balance awaiting the
leader's order to fire, or recover arms. The latter order
came. He then said excitedly: "Now will you talk?" But I
remained silent.

This performance was repeated. He became filled with
wrath, and commanded his men, the third time, "Make ready!
Aim!" It looked surely as though my time had come. At
this moment, a man in military garb, and armed with a sword,
came running from the camp near the grocery. When near
enough to to be heard, he cried out, "Hold on!"

The men dropped their peices, and there was respite for me
again. As he approached he demanded, "What are you
doing?"

The officer who had been abusing me, replied with a profane
epithet, "I am going to kill this Mormon!"

The other officer ordered him to take his men to the camp.

As he did not move readily, his superior drew his sword,
stepped in front of him, and declared with an oath, if he did
not move at once he would take his head from his shoulders.
His tone and manner indicated that he meant business, and
the captain moved off with his men at once.

The officer who released me, declared that the other was
drunk and did not know what he was doing. He asked me
many questions similar to what the other had done, but in a
gentlemanly manner, and I answered them frankly and truly.
His heart was softened towards me. He bade me go on my
way, and added, "Mr. Young if you are ever in trouble in
this war, and can do so, send for me, and you shall not be hurt,
unless it is over my dead body. I made a memorandum of
his name, military title, etc., but regret to say that in my
many moves since have lost it.

Again was the prophetic promise of my mother fulfilled,
and my life lengthened out for some wise purpose. Brother
Decker and I went on home. He immediately removed to
Far West, Caldwell County.

CHAPTER VI.

WARNED TO LEAVE THE COUNTRY OR REUOUNCE "MORMON-
ISM" — WIFE AND CHILDREN THREATENED—A BOY'S
PLUCK—FORCED TO FLEE FOR OUR LIVES—PROPERTY
CONFISCATED—BATTLE OF CROOKED RIVER—PROVIDEN-
TIALLY SAVED—FAR WEST BESIEGED—ESCAPE TO IOWA
—PURSUED—PROVIDENTIAL SNOW STORM.

In a day or two after my return home, Mr. Richard Weld-
ing, of whom I had bought my farm, came to me, accompanied
by three or four others. He gave me warning to leave the
country at once.

I asked him why I must leave, saying: "Have I not bought
my land, and paid you for it? Have I not attended to my
own business?"

He replied: "Mr. Young, we do not want you to leave.
You are a good neighbor and citizen, and if you will only be
man enough to renounce Joe Smith and your religion, we
want you to remain with us, and I will protect you in your
rights. The Mormons must all leave the country, and if you
do not renounce them, you must go too."

I paid no attention to this warning.

Three or four days after this occurrence, four men rode up
in front of my house, when I happened to be away, called
Sister Young to the door, and again gave warning that we
had better leave.

By her side stood our little boy, Joseph W. One of the
men, using an oath, ordered him to go into the house or he
would blow his brains out. The boy stepped back, without
his mother noticing what he was doing, took my rifle, which
was standing in the room, and, before he had attracted her
attention, was leveling it on the threatener. She quietly told
him not to fire, as they would certainly be killed if he did.

He obeyed, but manifested considerable beligerency for one
of his age.

About five days after this warning, early in the morning, I looked up the road towards Gallatin, and saw a man on horseback coming towards my house at full speed. As he rode up he inquired: "Is your name Young?"

I answered that it was.

He continued: "I have rode from Gallatin to inform you that, in two or three hours, there will be a company of forty men here, who assert that if they find you here, they will fasten you and your family in your house and burn it down. For God's sake, if you value your own life and the lives of your wife and children, do not be here an hour from now. I have come to give you this warning as a friend. Should it be found out that I have done so, I might lose my own life!"

I thanked him for his kindness, and he rode off rapidly towards Gallatin. I told Sister Young to prepare to leave at once, then attached my team to a light spring wagon, put a bed, a few cooking utensils, a trunk of clothing, and some food for the day into it. I got my wife, my four children, William, Harriet, Joseph and John into the wagon, fastened up the house and started for Far West.

I expected to return and get my goods. The next day I obtained some teams and started for my goods. I found the road strongly guarded, and the Missourians threatened to kill me if I went on. I never obtained goods, cows nor anything that I had left on my place.

This left my family very destitute, in common with others of the Saints who had been treated in like manner.

I had previously driven a fine yoke of oxen and a new milch cow to Far West, thinking I might possibly want to remove there; but Clark's army drove my oxen into camp and butchered them for beef. I was promised pay for them, but, of course, never received anything but the promise.

This was in October, 1838. I remained in Far West doing whatever was necessary for the protection of the Saints. I was on guard much of the time.

Major Seymour Brunson directed Brother A. P. Rockwood and myself to take our horses and go out two miles north of Far West and patrol the country every night. If we saw a man, or company of men coming towards Far West, we were

2*

ordered to hail them and demand the countersign. If necessary, to make this demand the second time, when, if not given, we were to fire on them. When we arrived on the ground where we were to perform our duties, Brother Rockwood and I separated, taking different directions. It was a moonlight night. I was on the edge of a prairie with my eye along the road, when I discovered a company of mounted men coming over a swell of the prairie. I retired into the timber and took a station behind the trunk of a large tree, under the shadow of its branches, and twenty or thirty yards from the road. As the company came opposite to me, I demanded the countersign twice, as I had been ordered to do. As they paid no attention to me, I made ready to fire, intending to shoot the leader, when a strong and sudden impression came over me to hail again. I did so, and ordered them to halt. This time the leader recognized my voice, and, turning towards me, asked: "Is that you, Brother Lorenzo?" I also recognized the man as Brother Lyman Wight, and, as I answered in the affirmative, rode up to his side. We were glad to meet each other, and I was very thankful that I had not obeyed orders. He was on his way from Diamond to Far West, with a company of men to assist the Saints there.

Soon after this occurrence, I returned to Far West. I told Sister Young that I hoped to get one good night's sleep. For three weeks I had not had my clothes off to lay down, and I felt much worn.

Perhaps I had slept two hours, when I was awakened by the bass drum sounding an alarm on the public square. I was soon out to see what was the matter. There were five men on the square, of whom I inquired the cause of the alarm. They informed me that two of the brethren had been taken prisoners by the mob on Crooked River, tried by a court martial that day, and condemned to be shot the coming morning at eight o'clock. A company of men was wanted to go and rescue them.

Preparations were soon made, and in a short time, about 40 mounted men, under the command of David W. Patten, were ready to start. We kept the road to a ford on Crooked River, twenty miles distant, where we expected to find the mob.

Just as the day was breaking we dismounted, about a mile from the ford, tied our horses, and left Brother Isaac Decker to watch them.

We marched down the road some distance, when we heard the crack of a rifle. Brother Obanion, who was one step in advance of me fell. I assisted brother John P. Green, who was the captain of the platoon I belonged to, to carry him to the side of the road. We asked the Lord to preserve his life, laid him down, ran on and took our places again.

The man who shot Brother Obanion was a picket guard of the mob, who was secreted in ambush by the roadside. Captain Patten was ahead of the company.

As we neared the river the firing was somewhat lively. Captain Patten turned to the left of the road, with a part of the command; Captain Green and others turned to the right.

We were ordered to charge, which we did, to the bank of the river, when the enemy broke and fled.

I snapped my gun twice at a man in a white blanket coat. While engaged in repriming my gun, he got out of range,

A tall, powerful, Missourian sprang from under the bank of the river, and, with a heavy sword in hand, rushed towards one of the brethren, crying out, "Run, you devils, or die!"

The man he was making for was also armed with a sword, but was small and poorly calculated to withstand the heavy blows of the Missourian. He, however, succeded in defendhimself until I ran to his aid, and leveled my gun within two feet of his enemy, but it missed fire.

The Missourian turned on me. With nothing but the muzzle end of my rifle to parry his rapid blows, my situation was perilous. The man whom I had relieved, for some reason, did not come to the rescue. I succeeded in parrying the blows of my enemy until he backed me to the bank of the river. I could back no farther without going off the perpendicular bank, eight or ten feet above the water. In a moment I realized that my chances were very desperate. At this juncture the Missourian raised his sword, apparently throwing all his strength and energy into the act, as if intending to crush me with one desperate blow.

As his arm extended I saw a hand pass down the back of

his head and between his shoulders. There was no other person visible, and I have always believed that I saw the hand of the angel of the Lord interposed for my deliverance. The arm of my enemy was paralyzed, and I had time to extricate myself from the perilous situation I was in.

As soon as I had time to think, I felt that the inspiration of my mother's promise had been again verified. The appearance of the hand, to me, was real. I do not see how I could have been saved in the way I was, without a providential interference.

As soon as I was out of danger, my attention was drawn to brother David W. Patten, who lay on the ground a short distance from me, mortally wounded. We hitched a pair of horses to a wagon, put brother Patten and six other wounded men into it, and started for Far West.

A few miles from the battle ground we met the Prophet Joseph, with a carriage and a company of horsemen. The wounded were taken to their homes, and such care given them as circumstauces would allow.

Soon after our return to Far West, General Clark's army arrived before that city. In the evening after Joseph and Hyrum Smith and others had been taken prisoners, Hyrum Smith had the privilege of coming into Far West to see his family. From the spirit of General Clark and his army, he believed that, if they succeeded in taking the brethren who were in the Crooked River battle, they would be tried by a court martial and shot. !He and Rrother Brigham, and myself met on the public square. After counseling over the matter, it was decided that I, and others in the same situation, should start that night into the wilderness north, for the Des Moines River, in Iowa Territory. My brother, Phineas, being a good woodsman, was selected to pilot us.

The Saints in Far West had been so plundered by their enemies, that they had but little surplus to eat or wear.

I had on a very thin pair of pants. My wife took a sheet from the bed, and, with the assistance of some of the neighbors, hastily made me a pair of drawers. These I afterwards gave to my brother Phineas, as he seemed to suffer more with the cold than I did. Our bedding was as scanty as our clothing.

We left Far West that night, and took no food with us. We arrived about sunrise in the morning, at Adam-Ondi-Ahman, twenty-two miles from Far West. We needed some breakfast, and stopped in a clump of hazel brush, and sent one of the party to the house of Brother Gardiner Snow, to tell him our situation. He said he had not much to eat, but would do the best he could. He brought us a very good supply of stewed Missouri pumpkin and milk. Our keen appetites made this seem a very good breakfast.

There we obtained fifty pounds of chopped corn. With this meagre supply of food we continued on our journey. From the first, it was evident that we must be very saving of our food supply. We rationed on eight ounces of this meal, per man, each day. It was mixed with water, without any salt, baked in a cake before the fire, and carefully divided out.

The second day, as night was approaching, we struck the edge of a prairie, which was about four miles across. As our horses were weary, we stopped a short time to rest, when one Irvine Hodge overtook us. He informed us that General Clark, having learned of our departure, had sent a troop of sixty cavalrymen in pursuit; that they were only a few miles behind, and on our trail. Their orders were to bring us dead or alive. We had thought of camping on the spot, but concluded to cross the prairie at once. This we accomplished, and camped in the timber. In the night, snow commenced falling. It appeared to come down in sheets instead of flakes. In the morning it was about a foot and a half deep. Some of the company, at first, regretted this, but others saw and felt that the hand of the Lord was in it. My brother, Phineas, at once declared that it was the means of our deliverance. We started on and the wind began to blow. Our tracks were completely covered soon after they were made.

We afterwards learned that our pursuers camped on the opposite side of the prairie from us, where we had rested. In the morning they tried to find our trail, but finding it impossible to do so, gave up pursuit.

Thus we were saved from our enemies by a friendly interposition of the elements in our behalf.

We were fifteen days on our journey from Far West to the Des Moines River. The last three days we were without food. After the snow fell, our horses had to subsist on what they could find above it.

The brush had soon made my thin pants unavailable for covering my legs in the neighborhood of the knees. The fragments were tied up with small hickory withes. When we arrived near a house, on the Des Moines, I remained in the woods while one of my companions went to the house and obtained a pair of pants, that I might be presentable.

On this trip it seemed as though both men and animals had a wonderful power of enduring cold, hunger and fatigue. I am constrained, after more than forty years have passed away, to acknowledge a special providence in our deliverance.

I have drawn on my memory for the facts of this narative, and think that they are correct; but there may be some errors in dates, and in the succession of events.

AN INSTANCE OF DIVINE INTERPOSITION.

BY ELDER WILLIAM BUDGE.

VISIT TO SCOTLAND—MEET OLD FRIENDS- -RETURN TO LIVER-
POOL—ABOUT TO GO BY STEAMER TO BRISTOL—A VOICE
WARNS ME NOT TO GO—TURN BACK—SHORT OF MONEY—
MEANS PROVIDENTIALLY PROVIDED—JOURNEY TO PORTS-
MOUTH—SEQUEL TO THE WARNING—THE STEAMER
WRECKED.

I HAD been laboring in the Southampton Conference, England, as a missionary for about two years, when I obtained
permission to visit my relatives in Scotland. It was in the
latter part of the summer of 1853.

Accompanied by an Elder named Armstrong, who was
going to Liverpool, I embarked at Portsmouth, on the steam-
ship *Duke of Cornwall*, bound for that port, on the morning of the 8th of August.

Shortly after starting, we passed the British fleet, lying off
Spithead, preparing for a grand review, to take place on the
following Thursday; which Queen Victoria was expected to
attend. The scene was both novel and intese sting, as we
passed near the assembled and decorated ships.

Passing the Isle of Wight, of which we had a good view,
we called at Plymouth, Falmouth, and Penzance, before
reaching Liverpool, passing also the celebrated Eddystone
Lighthouse.

We reached Liverpool at two p. m., on the 10th, and I
sailed for Glasgow within two hours afterwards. On board
the Scotch steamer, I was pleased to find an old acquaintance,

named George Turnbull, who was at that time a clerk in the Church office at Liverpool, and on his way, like myself, to visit his home and friends.

Brother Turnbull and I heard the gospel about the same time, in the same city, (Glasgow) and became members of the same branch of the Church; he being baptized first. This young man was a scholar, and possessed of much natural ability, and for some time, was a good Saint, but he would not run the race; he eventually fell into transgression, denied the faith, and was lost.

There were also on board the vessel, Elder Fullmer, pastor of the Liverpool Conference, and wife, and Elder John O. Angus, President of the Shropshire Conference. I was well acquainted with the latter; he was a faithful missionary, and a quiet, humble, and inoffensive man. He labored for a long time in the St. George Temple, and died some time ago.

Such company was very agreeable, but the night was somewhat stormy, and we did not reach Glasgow until two p. m. next day.

During this trip, I visited my relatives in Glasgow, Lanark, and elsewhere, and also the Saints in a district of the conference where I had formerly labored. I felt truly grateful to the Lord for all His goodness unto me, in preserving me while struggling hard in several new fields of labor to which I had been allotted, since I first left home and began my labors as a missionary.

On the first day of September, taking leave of my friends, I embarked on a steam vessel for Liverpool. Elder John O. Angus was also a passenger, and I, therefore, had good company during a very stormy passage. Arriving at Liverpool, we called at the Church office, Wilton Street, and lodged at the house of Elder A. F. Macdonald, president of the conference.

I intended to go by sea from Liverpool to Bristol, and by land to Salisbury, on my way back to Portsmouth, as I had not means enough to go through by railroad conveyance. I had explained this to Brother Angus, and on the morning after our arrival in Liverpool, I bade him good by, and walked down to the docks, carying my carpet sack and a number of books, which I had brought with me from home. This was on the third day of September, 1853.

A number of people were waiting to go on board the same steam vessel I intended to take. The steamer at the time was taking in freight at the opposite side of the dock, and would call for us, so we were informed, in a short time.

While standing looking at the vessel, a voice, loud and distinct, said: "Do not go on board." I was startled, and looked around, but there was no one near. Although I turned hastily, I did not really expect to see any one who might have spoken. It was, I felt, a revelation; I was impressed with the divine force, and I lifted my satchel preparatory to leaving, but suddenly I thought of my want of means, and began to wonder whether I had not been deceived by my imagination. I put down my satchel again, just as the ship was nearing that part of the dock where the passengers were waiting. My condition tempted me. I was in doubt for a moment. I began to reason; but faith triumphed. I felt sure that it was a warning, and, lifting my baggage, left the dock for the Lime Street Station, as the people who had been waiting passed into the steamer.

Once decided, there was no further trouble, and I began to consider how I could reach Portsmouth. When I entered the station, I had concluded to take the first third-class train to Birmingham. At that time, I had no acquaintances there, and wished to hurry on, trusting that the way would be opened up as my necessities required; such having been the case many times before. The Lord had prepared the way in times past, and I had faith that He would help me then sufficiently.

I was one of those young and very inexperienced Elders, sent into the missionary field literally without purse or scrip. Elder George B. Wallace, at that time one of the presidency of the Church in Europe, sent me with several others into Cumberland County, in the North of England, where there were no Saints until we were instrumental in the hands of the Lord in bringing some to a knowledge of the truth.

It was a hard country, and we had a rough experience. In less than three months, three Elders out of five returned home; but Elder Thomas Wallace, now of Weber County, and I remained until the Lord called us somewhere else.

I have been in many new fields of labor since, without money and without friends until the Lord raised them up, but never among a people so ignorant, and unimpressionable as the people we could obtain access to in the North of England. In comparison, my prospects, as I walked into the Lime Street Station, were not at all discouraging, but as I entered, there stood Brother Angus, who was waiting for a train to take him to Shrewsbury.

He was surprised to see me, and I was a little abashed, as I felt somewhat delicate about giving him an explanation. Although satisfied myself, I had some misgivings about satisfying him. I told him, however, what had happened, and, to my relief, he said, putting his hand on my shoulder, "You have done just right, and you will see the hand of God in this."

A third-class train, I learned, would not leave until next morning, so I lodged with Brother Turnbull, who had returned to Liverpool.

The next day I went to Birmingham, and there learned that a cheap excursion train would leave for Bristol at five p. m. Bristol—going by land—was not directly on my way, but the fare being low, and going from there to Warminster and Salisbury, I was likely to reach Portsmouth sooner than any other way.

In the cars, I made the acquaintance of a lady and gentleman also going to Bristol, to visit some relatives they had in that town. After an interesting conversation they invited me to take lunch with them, which was very acceptable, and on our arrival at Bristol, they pressed me to accompany them to their friend's house, where I remained all night, being warmly received and well treated.

I had not quite a dollar in my possession, and I acknowledge the hand of the Lord in thus opening up the way for me.

On reaching Warminster next day at six p. m., I had only twelve cents left, and a heavy carpet sack, which I took to a carrier who made occasional trips with freight to Salisbury, and I started at once to walk to the latter place, distant twenty-two miles.

It was evening and the weather pleasant, and the distance nothing unusual for a missionary, but I made a mistake by starting out too fast, perspired, got tired, and was obliged to take lodging at a small way-side inn, which cost me eight cents. I slept without supper and resumed my journey without breakfast the next morning, but thanking the Lord for good health and spirits.

On reaching Salisbury, where I was a perfect stranger, I walked into the town with the intention of inquiring for Latter-day Saints, a few of whom I understood lived there. My first inquiry was of a little boy, who quickly answered "Yes, my mother is one," and at once offered to conduct me to his home, which we soon reached, and to which I was warmly welcomed.

On passing through the streets, I saw, posted upon the walls, announcements of an excursion trip to Southampton and Portsmouth, fare two shillings and six pence, or sixty-two cents in our money. Reflecting upon the means of obtaining such a sum without being obliged to write and wait for it, we reached the house of my guide's mother.

From the boy's statement that his mother was a "Mormon," I got the impression that his father, if he had one, was not, which I found to be correct. His father was not very friendly, but his mother was a very earnest Saint, and a very thoughtful and kind one, as while I sat taking some refreshments which she had hastily prepared, she brought and gave me a piece of money, the exact amount necessary to procure my ticket to Portsmouth. I again thanked the Lord, and explained to my kind sister what her gift would enable me to do. The boy had in the meantime, by her instructions, brought my carpet sack, and I was ready to continue my journey.

I reached Portsmouth on the 7th day of September, and while there on the 9th, I read in the newspaper of the total wreck of the steam vessel, on which I was about to sail from Liverpool, when I was warned by the Lord not to go on board the ship.

MY LAST MISSION TO THE SANDWICH ISLANDS.

BY WM. W. CLUFF.

CHAPTER I.

ELDERS CALLED HOME FROM THE SANDWICH ISLANDS—NATIVE ELDERS LEFT TO PRESIDE—GIBSON'S ARRIVAL IN SALT LAKE—JOINS THE CHURCH—ASKS FOR A MISSION TO THE SANDWICH ISLANDS—HIS DEEP-LAID SCHEME—LEADING ASTRAY THE HAWAIIAN SAINTS—FIVE ELDERS SENT TO INVESTIGATE—ARRIVAL AT THE SANDWICH ISLANDS—ATTEMPT TO GO ASHORE IN A BOAT—CAPSIZED IN THE SURF—ELDER LORENZO SNOW LOST—AFTER A LONG SEARCH, FOUND UNDER THE BOAT—EFFORTS TO RESUSCITATE HIM—RESTORED TO LIFE ONE HOUR AFTER BEING DROWNED.

IN the summer and autumn of 1857, a United States army was marching towards Utah, evidently with hostile intentions towards its people. It was thought wisdom, by the authorities of the Church, to concentrate the strength of the Saints for any emergency, by calling home the Elders that were on foreign missions.

When the last of the Elders from Utah left the Sandwich Islands, on the 1st of May, 1858, the care of the Saints on each of the islands was entrusted to a native Elder. Kailihûne was appointed to preside over the gathering place on Lanai. He was among the first fruits of the labors of the Elders, and for a long time had been very efficient and faithful.

During our difficulties with the government Walter M. Gibson, an adventurer, came to Utah. His ostensible object was to induce President Young, and the general Church authorities, to remove our people *en masse*, to the East India Islands. He painted, in glowing colors, the splendid facilities and opportunities those islands offered for immigration and colonization, by an enterprising and industrious people like the Latter-day Saints.

In his ignorance, he supposed that the object of the founder and leaders of the Church was to found a powerful and independent nation. The object of these schemes was, evidently, his own personal aggrandizement.

It had, no doubt, been a favorite project of his, for years, to found a government somewhere on the islands of the Pacific Ocean. Failing in his scheme for the removal of the Church, some other plan must be devised for the accomplishment of his cherished purpose.

He professed to become a convert to our faith, and was baptized into the Church. He then requested to be sent on a mission to the Polynesian Islands. He desired a roving commission from the Presidency of the Church, authorizing him to travel and preach, on any or all of the islands, in the Pacific Ocean.

Before leaving Salt Lake City, Mr. Gibson made it a specialty to converse with the Elders who had lately returned from the Sandwich Islands. He sought to be well informed on the general condition of the islands, the customs, traditions, and general character of the natives, and, especially did he seek to be well informed as to the numbers, organization, location, and general condition of the native Saints. His object, in this, developed afterwards.

When he left Utah he went directly to the Sandwich Islands. He soon found some of the Saints, and represented to them, that he had been sent by President Young, not only to take charge of the mission on those islands, but to preside over all the churches that might be raised up on any of the Pacific islands, and, in that capacity, that he was equal to, and entirely independent of President Young.

The native Saints had been left about two years to themselves. They were naturally simple and credulous, and it was easy to impose upon them.

As soon as Mr. Gibson acquired some knowledge of the native language, he commenced traveling among the branches of the Church, and grafted on to the gospel, many of the old traditio.s and superstitions of the Hawaiians. He reorganized the Church, or, more properly speaking, reconstructed it in accordance with his own notions, throughout the islands.

He was one of those characters, of whom the apostle Peter warned the Saints in his day, "and through covetousness shall they with feigned words make merchandise of you." He ordained twelve apostles, and charged them one hundred and fifty dollars each for initiating them into the office, and charged High Priests, Seventies, etc, proportionately, according to the presumed importance of the offices.

By this and other impositions, he succeeded in raising sufficient means for the purchase of one half of the island of Lanai. Some years before the Elders had leased the same tract of land, of Halelea, a native chief, for a temporary gathering place for the Saints.

Mr. Gibson represented to the Saints that he was securing the land for them, but that it would have to be deeded to him for them.

For the accomplishment of his purpose, concentration and organization were necessary. He continued to gather the Saints to Lanai. There he organized all the males, old and young, into companions, and daily drilled them in the art of war. He informed them that, as soon as they were properly disciplined, it was his intention to build or purchase a vessel, equip it, and sail for one of the South Sea Islands. He would seek a favorable opportunity, conquer the natives, leave some of his disciplined men in charge of the conquered territory, and fill up his depleted ranks with raw recruits.

In this way, he designed to conquer one island after another, until he organized a large fleet, and subjugated all the Polynesian Islands. Thus he hoped to realize his wildest dreams by organizing, as he expressed it, "One great grand empire," that would be able to take its place among the leading nations of the earth.

His every act from the time of his arrival in Utah, had been designed for his own aggrandizement. He had learned nothing of the spirit and power of the gospel. The Lord is establishing His kingdom, and he was fighting against it. If he has not already done so, he will yet realize the truth of the saying of the Savior, in his teachings, when, on his earthly mission, he likened the Kingdom of God to a stone, and said, "And whosoever shall fall on this stone shall be broken: but on whomsoever it may fall, it will grind him to powder."

Notwithstanding the Saints had been gradually led astray by Mr. Gibson, they felt that his teachings and practices were not the same as those of the Elders who had labored among them before his coming.

Fearing they might be deceived, some eight of the native Elders wrote to brethren in Utah who had labored for many years among them. They stated some of the facts concerning Mr. Gibson's course, and asked for advice. This communication was translated and submitted to President Young.

The First Presidency decided that Apostles E. T. Benson and Lorenzo Snow should visit the islands, and that Elders Joseph. F. Smith, Alma L. Smith, and myself, who had previously been on missions to the islands and understood the native language, should accompany them.

We arrived at Honolulu, the capital of the islands, about the 27th of March, 1864. On the 29th we sailed for Lahaina, on the schooner, *Nettie Merrill*, Captain Fisher, for the island of Maui, a distance of about ninety miles from Honolulu. On the morning of the 31st of March, we came to anchor about one mile from the mouth of the little harbor of Lahaina.

Apostles Ezra T. Benson, Lorenzo Snow, Brother Alma L. Smith, and myself, got into the small boat to go ashore. Brother Joseph F. Smith, as he afterwards stated, had some misgivings about going in that boat, but the manifestation was not sufficiently strong to indicate any general accident. He preferred to remain on board the vessel, until the boat returned.

The boat started for the shore. It contained some barrels and boxes, the captain, a white man, two or three native passengers, and the boat's crew, who were also natives.

The entrance to the harbor is a very narrow passage between coral reefs, and when the sea is rough it is very dangerous, on account of the breakers. Where the vessel lay the sea was not rough, but only presented the appearance of heavy swells rolling to the shore.

As we approached the reef it was evident to me, that the surf was running higher than we anticipated. I called the captain's attention to the fact. We were running quartering across the waves, and I suggested that we change our course so as to run at right angles with them. He replied, that he did not think there was any danger, and our course was not changed. We went but little farther, when a heavy swell struck the boat and carried us before it about fifty yards. When the swell passed it left us in a trough between two huge waves.

It was too late to retrieve our error, and we must run our chances. When the second swell struck the boat, it raised the stern so high that the steersman's oar was out of the water, and he lost control of the boat. It rode on the swell a short distance, and swung around just as the wave began to break up. We were almost instantly capsized, into the dashing, foaming sea.

I felt no concern for myself about drowning, for while on my former mission I had learned to swim and sport in the surf of those shores.

The last I remembered of Brother Snow, as the boat was going over I saw him seize the upper edge of it with both hands. Fearing that the upper edge of the boat, or the barrels, might hit and injure me as the boat was going over, I plunged head foremost into the water. After swimming a short distance, I came to the surface without being strangled or injured.

The boat was bottom upwards, and barrels, hats, and umbrellas were floating in every direction. I swam to the boat and as there was nothing to cling to on the bottom, I reached under and seized the edge of it.

About the same time, brother Benson came up near me, and readily got hold of the boat.

The natives soon appeared, and swam about quite unconcerned for their own safety. Brother Alma L. Smith came up on the opposite side of the boat from brother Benson and myself. He was considerably strangled, but succeeded in securing a hold on the boat.

A short time afterwards the captain was discovered, about fifty yards from us. Two of his sailors swam to his assistance, and, one on each side, succeeded in keeping him on the surface, although life was apparently extinct.

Nothing yet had been seen of Brother Snow, although the natives had been swimming and diving in every direction in search of him. We were only about one fourth of a mile from the shore. The people, as soon as they discovered our circumstances, manned a life boat and hurried to the rescue.

We were taken into the boat, when the crew wanted to row for the shore, and pick up the captain on the way. We told them that one of our friends was yet missing, and we did not want to leave, as long as there was any possibility of a chance to render him assistance. We discovered that a second boat had left the shore, and could reach the captain as soon as the one we were in. Seeing this, the crew of the boat we were in, consented to remain and assist us.

The captain was taken ashore, and, by working over him for some time, was brought to life.

The life of Captain Fisher would not, probably, have been much endangered, except for a sack of four or five hundred dollars in silver which he held in his hand. This he clung to with great tenacity. When the boat capsized the weight of it took him at once to the bottom. The natives dove and brought him up, still clinging to the sack. When his vitality was restored, the first thing he inquired about was the money; intimating to the natives, with peculiar emphasis, that it would not have been healthy for them to have lost it.

Brother Snow had not yet been discovered, and the anxiety was intense. The natives were, evidently, doing all in their power.

Finally, one of them, in edging himself around the capsized boat, must have felt Brother Snow with his feet and pulled him, at least partly, from under it, as the first I saw of Brother Snow was his hair floating upon the water as the native was dragging him through the water around one end of the capsized boat. As soon as we got him into our boat, we told the boatmen to pull for the shore with all possible speed. His body was stiff, and life was evidently extinct.

Brother Alma L. Smith and myself were sitting side by side. We laid Brother Snow across our laps, and, on the way to shore, we quietly administered to him and asked the Lord to spare his life, that he might return to his family and home.

On reaching the shore, we carried him a little way, to some large empty barrels that were lying on the sandy beach. We laid him, face downwards, on one of these, and rolled him back and forth until we succeeded in getting the water that he had swallowed out of him.

During this time, a number of persons came down from the town; among them was Mr. E. P. Adams, a merchant. Al were willing to do what they could. We washed Brother Snow's face with camphor, furnished by Mr. Adams. We did not only what was customary in such cases, but also what the spirit seemed to whisper to us.

After working over him for some time, without any indications of returning life, the bystanders said that nothing more could be done for him. But we did not feel like giving him up, and still prayed and worked over him, with an assurance that the Lord would hear and answer our prayers.

Finally we were impressed to place our mouth over his and make an effort to inflate his lungs, alternately blowing in and drawing out the air, imitating, as far as possible, the natural process of breathing. This we persevered in until we succeeded in inflating his lungs. After a little, there were very faint indications of returning vitality. A slight wink of the eye, which, until then, had been open and deathlike, and a very faint rattle in the throat, were the first symptoms of returning life. These grew more and more distinct, until consciousness was fully restored.

When this result was reached, it must have been fully an hour after the capsizing of the boat. A Portuguese man, living in Lahaina, who, from the first, rendered us much assistance, invited us to take Brother Snow to his house. There being no Saints in the place, we gladly accepted his kind offer.

Every possible attention was given to Brother Snow's comfort.

Persons in danger and excitement, often see things a little differently.   The following is Apostle Snow's account of the capsizing of the boat:

"As we were moving along within some half a mile from the point where we expected to land, my attention was suddenly arrested by Captain Fisher calling to the oarsmen, in a voice which denoted some alarm, 'Hurry up! hurry up!'   I quickly discovered the cause of alarm.

"A short distance behind us, I saw an immense surf, thirty or forty feet high, rushing towards us swifter than a race horse.   We had scarcely a moment for reflection before the huge mass was upon us.   In an instant our boat, with its contents, as though it were only a feather, was hurled into the briny water, and we were under this rolling, seething, mountain wave.

"This was certainly unexpected.   It took me by surprise. I think, however, that I soon comprehended the situation: that we were in the midst of the turbulent waters, a quarter of a mile from the shore, without much probability of receiving human aid.

"I felt confident, however, that there would be some way of escape; that the Lord would provide the means, for it was not possible that my life and mission were thus to terminate. This reliance on the Lord banished fear, and inspired me with hope up to the last moment of consciousness.

"Having been somewhat subject to fainting spells, I believe that after a few moments in the water, I must have fainted, as I did not suffer the pain common in the experience of drowning persons.   I had been in the water only a few moments, until I lost consciousness.

"The first I knew afterwards, I was on shore receiving the kind and tender attentions of my brethren.   The first recollection I have of returning consciousness, was seeing a very small light, the smallest maginable.   This soon disappeared, and I was again in total darkness.   Again it appeared, much larger than before, then sank away and left me, as before, in forgetfulness.   Thus it continued to come and go, until, finally,

I recognized, as I thought, persons whispering, and soon after I asked in a feeble whisper, 'What is the matter?'

"I immediately recognized the voice of Elder Cluff, as he replied, 'You have been drowned; the boat upset in the surf.' Quick as lightning, the scene of our disaster flashed upon my mind. I immediately asked, 'Are you brethren all safe?' The emotion that was awakened in my bosom by the answer of Elder Cluff, will remain as long as life continues: 'Brother Snow, we are all safe.'

"I·rapidly recovered, and very soon was able to walk and accompany the brethren to our lodgings."

As soon as Brother Snow was out of danger, it occurred to me that I had better return to the vessel.

As I reached the deck, by the rope ladder over its side, I saw, at a glance, that Brother Smith was under great anxiety of mind.

We were both under an intensity of feeling, which men usually experience only a few times in their lives. Brother Smith had been informed by a native that the captain and an elderly white man were drowned. The latter, he supposed to be Brother Benson, hence his great anxiety.

My own nervous system was strung up to an extreme tension by the events of the past two hours. When I told Brother Smith that all were safe, the sudden revulsion of feeling almost overcame him. We rejoiced together that through a merciful Providence, and the faith that had been bestowed upon us, we were all alive.

CHAPTER II.

JOURNEY TO LANAI—MEET MR. GIBSON—REVERENCE OF NATIVES FOR HIM—HIS SPEECH AND ASSUMPTION—ELDER JOSEPH F. SMITH'S REPLY—ELDER SNOW'S PROPHECY— MR. GIBSON CUT OFF THE CHURCH—ELDER SNOW'S PROPHECY FULFILLED—ADVISED TO SELECT A NEW GATHERING PLACE—A VISION—SUITABLE PLACE POINTED OUT.

ON the 2nd of April, Brother Snow had so far recovered his strength, that it was thought best to pursue our journey. We hired some natives to take us in an open boat across the channel, sixteen miles, to Lanai. We arrived at the landing place, three miles from the village, just at dark. We sent a messenger to Mr. Gibson, with the request that he would send down some saddle horses for us to ride up in the morning.

Early the following morning, April 3rd, the horses were ready for us. An hour's ride over a rough, rocky road brought us to the settlement. Our reception by Mr. Gibson, and most of the native Saints, was cool and very formal. Many improvements had been made since our last visit, that were praiseworthy, and reflected great credit on Mr. Gibson.

After breakfast, Apostles Benson and Snow engaged in conversation with Mr. Gibson on the affairs of the mission.

That day and the following, were principally spent in laboring with Mr. Gibson and the native Elders, to get them, if possible, to see the condition they were in. During this time, Brothers Joseph F. Smith, Alma L. Smith and myself, took a ride around the valley accompanied by Mr. Gibson's daughter, as our guide. About one-half of a mile from Mr. Gibson's residence, was a large rock, the top several feet above the ground. Mr. Gibson had a chamber cut into this rock, in which he had deposited a Book of Mormon, and other things, and called it the corner stone of a great temple,

which would be erected there. A frame work of poles had
been constructed, in a circular form around this rock, and
this was covered with brush.

Mr. Gibson, by appealing to the pagan superstitions of the
natives, made them believe that this spot was sacred, and if
any person touched it, he would be struck dead.

So much faith had the daughter of Mr. Gibson in the
teachings of her father, that she related, apparently in good
faith, the circumstance of a hen flying upon the boothe, and
immediately falling down dead.

Notwithstanding the protest of Miss Gibson, that it was
very dangerous to do so, we went inside of the brush structure, and examined the rock and came out unharmed.

We were further informed that Mr. Gibson had succeeded
in surrounding his own person and residence with such a
halo of sacredness in the minds of the natives, that they
always entered his house on their hands and knees.

This was repeated on other occasions. It was the old
customary way, in which the natives had been in the habit of
paying respect to their kings, and the custom had been revived
by Mr. Gibson, in order to increase his personal prestige.

We had previously learned that the Saints would assemble
in conference on the 6th of April. At ten o'clock, a. m.,
they had assembled in the meeting house. We all started
to go in, when Mr. Gibson made some excuse for returning to
his house. We went and took our seats on the stand. The
house was well filled. In a few minutes Mr. Gibson made
his appearance. As soon as he entered the door, the entire
congregation instantly arose to their feet, and remained standing until he was seated on the stand. The execution of this
act of reverence evinced long and careful training.

Mr. Gibson had, doubtless, delayed his entrance, to make a
fitting opportunity for this exhibition. He entirely ignored
the presence of the Apostles, and, after the people were
seated, arose and gave out the opening hymn. This act gave
evidence, at once, that he had no proper idea of the organization and authority of the Priesthood. Seeing this,
President Benson called on me to pray.

Without giving any time for consultation, as soon as the second hymn was sung, Mr. Gibson arose to his feet and commenced to address the congregation, in substance as follows: "My dear red-skinned brethren, sisters and friends, I presume you are all wondering, and anxious to know why these strangers have come so suddenly among us, without giving us any notice of their coming. I will assure you of one thing, my red-skinned friends, when I find out, I will be sure to let you know, for I am your father, and will protect you in your rights.

"These strangers may say they are your friends, but let me remind you how, when they lived here, years ago, they lived upon your very scanty substance. Did they make any such improvements as you see I have made? Did I not come here and find you without a father, poor, and discouraged? Did I not gather you together here, and make all these improvements that you to-day enjoy?

"Now, you, my red-skinned friends, must decide who your friend and father is; whether it is these strangers, or I, who have done so much for you."

When he took his seat, President Benson requested Brother Joseph F. Smith to talk, rather intimating that it was desirable to speak on general principles, and that he need not feel bound to notice all that Mr. Gibson had said.

It seemed impossible for any man to speak with greater power and demonstration of the Spirit. He referred the Saints to the labors of Brother George Q. Cannon, and the first Elders who brought them the gospel.

He reminded them of facts with which the older Saints were well acquainted—the great disadvantage the Elders labored under, and the privations they suffered in first preaching the gospel on the islands. How they slept in their then miserable huts, and lived as they lived; how they traveled on foot, in storms, and in bad weather, from village to village, and from house to house, exposing health and life ; how they went destitute of clothing, and what they had been in the habit of considering the necessaries of life, to bring them the blessings of the gospel, without money and without price.

He asked by what right Mr. Gibson called himself the father of the people, and the Elders who faithfully labored to establish them in the gospel strangers.

The spirit and power that accompanied Brother Smith's remarks astonished the Saints and opened their eyes. They began to see how they had been imposed upon. Every word he spoke found a response in their hearts, as was plainly manifest by their eager looks and animated countenances.

There was another meeting in the afternoon, in which Apostles Benson and Snow addressed the Saints. Their remarks were interpreted by Elder Joseph F. Smith.

On the 7th, there was a meeting in the forenoon. A Priesthood meeting was appointed for the evening, and the conference adjourned *sine die*.

The meeting of the Priesthood in the evening was well attended, as it was understood that Mr. Gibson's course would be investigated. The complaints that were made by the native Elders, in the communication that led to our present mission, were read, and Mr. Gibson was called on to make answer to the charges.

In addition to nearly a repetition of his harangue at the meeting on the day previous, his reply consisted of a bombastic display of some letters of appointment, and recommendations from President Young, to which he attached large seals, bedecked with a variety of colored ribbons, to give them an air of importance, and official significance, in the eyes of the unsophisticated natives.

These papers he held up before the people, and, pointing to them said, with great emphasis, "Here is my authority, which I received direct from President Brigham Young. I don't hold myself accountable to these men!" meaning the Apostles and those who came with them.

Had there been no other proof of the wrong course of Mr. Gibson, that remark was sufficient to satisfy the brethren what their plain duty was, and they acted promptly in the matter.

Apostle E. T. Benson followed Mr. Gibson. He reviewed Mr. Gibson's past course, and showed that, in making merchandise of the offices of the Priesthood, introducing the former pagan superstitions of the people, for the purpose of obtaining power, and his idea of establishing a temporal and independent kingdom on the Pacific isles, were all in antagonism to the plan laid down in the gospel for the redemption of man.   The spirit manifested by Mr. Gibson proved that he was ignorant of the powers of the Priesthood, or that he ignored them for purely selfish motives.   What they had seen and heard since their arrival, proved that the complaints made by the native Elders, in their letters to Utah, were correct, as far as they went, but the half had not been told.

Brother Benson's remarks were interpreted, after which, it was motioned that Mr. Gibson's course be disapproved. When this was put to a vote, all but one of the native Elders voted against the motion.   This showed that Mr. Gibson still retained a strong hold on the minds of the Saints.

Notwithstanding this show of strong opposition, Brother Snow arose, and in his remarks prophesied that Mr. Gibson would see the time that not one of the Saints would remain with him.

Brother Joseph F. Smith remarked, that, among the scores of Elders who had labored on the islands, none had been so utterly wanting in the spirit and power of the gospel as to charge the Saints anything for conferring on them the blessings of the Priesthood, until Walter M. Gibson came, and had the presumption to claim that he had a right to ordain apostles and high priests, for a price—for money.

The Apostles informed Mr. Gibson and the Saints that, when they left the islands for home, Elder Joseph F. Smith would be left in charge of the mission.   That all those who wished to be considered in good standing in the Church should leave Lanai and return to their homes on the other islands, where the branches would be reorganized and set in order by the brethren who would be left for that purpose.

The next day we returned to Lahaina, where we held a council and cut Mr. Gibson off from the Church.   We returned to Honolulu, and, about eight days after, Apostles Snow and Benson took passage on the bark *Onward*, for San Francisco.

Brother Snow's prophecy was literally fulfilled.   The Saints all left Mr. Gibson and returned to their former homes, as they had been counseled to do. The last one to leave him was Kailihune, the Elder who had been left to preside over the place of gathering on Lanai.

He finally rejoined the Church. All the plans of Mr. Gibson were completely frustrated. He is a prominent example of the nothingness of man, when he attemps to battle against the kingdom of God.

When the Elders were called home, in 1858, there had not been time to do much in gathering the Saints. As Mr. Gibson had succeeded in obtaining a personal title to the land leased for that purpose, on the island of Lanai, brothers Benson and Snow advised the Elders who remained, to notice in their travels what appeared to them the best places for this purpose, that, when the time came for it, a good selection might be made.

On the island of Oahu, and near the sea shore, lived a white man by the name of Doharty. He did not belong to the Church, but was friendly to the Saints, and the Elders frequently shared his hospitality. Between his house and the sea beach was a piece of ground, where grew a very dense thicket of a large shrub of a peculiar growth. Through this were paths made by the people and their domestic animals. Into this thicket the Elders when there were in the habit of daily retiring to pray. One day when I was walking along one of these paths, I saw President Young approach me. Said he "This is the place to gather the native Saints to." He seemed to fully comprehend the surroundings, and in that easy, familiar way, so characteristic of him, indicated the advantages afforded for a settlement. No matter what my bodily condition might have been at that time, the apparent meeting was in the open air and the broad light of day. It was as real to me as any fact of my life. I saw the facilities of the place as he represented them, and ever afterwards, that appeared to me the best place on the islands for the gathering of the Saints.

We remained on the islands about six months before other Elders arrived from Utah, and we were released to return home. When we arrived in San Francisco, we met Elders F. A. Hammond, and George Nebeker, on their way to the Sandwich Islands. They had instructions to visit, and carefully examine all the islands, and make the best possible location that could be made available, to establish a place for the gathering of the Saints.

I was afterwards imformed, that they faithfully carried out their instructions, and at last decided that the place to which I have referred on the island of Oahu, was the best for the purpose. It was purchased, and many of the Saints are now gathered there.

They have an extensive sugar plantation, where labor is provided for them, and every possible facility is afforded for their advancement.

----•♦•----

A PROPHECY FULFILLED.

AN INCIDENT OF MISSIONARY EXPERIENCE.

BY B. F. JOHNSON.

CALLED ON A MISSION TO THE SANDWICH ISLANDS—JOURNEY BY THE SOUTHERN ROUTE—A PROPHECY—FEAR AFTER UTTERING IT—RESIDENCE IN HONOLULU—POLITICAL AND RELIGIOUS CONFLICT—THE KINGDOM IN JEOPARDY—DISSATISFACTION AMONG THE PEOPLE—LETTER TO THE KING FAVORABLY CONSIDERED—A DREAM—A PRINCE SENT BY THE KING TO ASK COUNSEL OF LATTER-DAY SAINT ELDERS —ADVICE ACCEPTED, AND THE KINGDOM SAVED—THE DREAM AND PROPHECY FULFILED TOGETHER.

WITH eight other Elders I was called by the General October Conference of 1852, on a mission to the Sandwich Islands. We went by what was then known as the Southern route to California, in order to sail from San Francisco.

In passing through the southern settlements of Utah, we were everywhere treated with kindness and respect. We were often invited to preach where we stopped for the night, or to spend the Sabbath. We were in company with many other Elders who were called to go on missions to China, Australia, Hindostan, Ceylon, and other places.

We all, alike, took part in the meetings, and shared the hospitality of the Saints. At Parowan we had an unusually good time, in a meeting of the Saints. The Spirit of the Lord rested greatly upon both hearers and speakers.

I was the last Elder called upon to speak, and only a few minutes were left for me to occupy. Being full of the good feeling and spirit of the meeting, I commenced, not only to bear my testimony to the truth, but to prophesy of the future of some of the sons of Zion who were then going forth as her ministers.

I predicted that, through faithfulness, the wisdom of heaven would increase with us; that while the wicked became weaker, the Elders of Israel would grow wiser; that the nations of the earth would begin to look towards Zion for counselors and statesmen, and that, if the Elders now going forth to the ends of the earth were true to their calling, they would not all fill their missions until some of them would be called upon to give counsel to some of the rulers of the lands to which they were sent.

After closing my prophecy and remarks, and I had time to ponder on what I had said, I began to doubt the possibility of my predictions being fulfilled, and began to be troubled in mind.

For a time I could not divest myself of the feeling, that my prediction was ill-timed and not by the spirit of the gospel. I would sometimes query if the brethren did not regard me as a false prophet, or, at least, as an enthusiast.

When we arrived on the Sandwich Islands, we found the work of the Lord progressing. The Elders who had been laboring there were greatly rejoiced to see us.

After a general mission conference, most of the brethren left Honolulu for their fields of labor on the different islands. I was left at this capital city, in charge of the foreign interests of the mission, to preside over a small branch of Saints, which had been gathered from the foreign residents on the islands, and to preach to the people as I might find opportunity. I also assisted Elders Lewis and Cannon, in raising funds for publishing the Book of Mormon in the native language.

Owing to the conflicting interests of political and religious parties in the Hawaiian kingdom, it was in a weak condition. The various missionary interests had nearly changed into political ones. Dr. Judd, one of the missionaries sent out by the American Board of Foreign Missions, had long been the king's prime minister. Another missionary, by the name of Armstrong, was Minister of Public Instruction, and other Americans filled the offices of Minister of Foreign Relations, Chief Justice, Attorney General, etc.

This missionary-political power began to cause great jealousy, especially in the case of Dr. Judd. Through his political advantages he had acquired much wealth, and, apparently by its use, raised himself up to be a power behind the throne, greater than the throne itself.

King Kamehameha III., like George the III., of England, had not reached a high standard of virtue, or political economy. It was said that, for money borrowed of Dr. Judd, he had given a mortgage on the royal palace.

As he had no children of his own he had adopted as next in succession, two sons of his sister, who were princes of the realm. About this time two projects were deeply agitating the public mind. One was the annexation of the islands to the United States, the other, a British protectorate over them. Neither of these projects suited the interests of the young princes, or pleased the majority of the people.

There appeared to be but one thing upon which nearly all the natives could agree, that was opposition to Dr. Judd as the king's prime minister. He was, of course, sustained by some of his fellow missionaries, but appeared to be detested by the majority of those around him. Petition after petition was sent to the king, asking for, and even demanding, his removal. The court house and other large halls were crowded with indignation meetings, to protest against his being retained in office.

It seemed, at times, as though the people would break out in tumult and insurrection, yet the king made no move to give them satisfaction, and, for many days, no answer was given to their petitions.

All this time I had been a careful observer, and had attended their meetings. I had previously written a lengthy letter to the king, explaining the gospel as now revealed and the object of our mission to the islands.

This letter he had caused to be published in the government journal, both in the English and Hawaiian languages. Such was the impression the reading of it made on his mind, that he sent, through the Minister of Foreign Relations, to say that he would give us an audience at his earliest convenience. Up to the time of which I am writing, he had not found the convenient opportunity.

In the midst of this political commotion, I, one night, dreamed that I stood upon an eminence near a large mountain. I saw below me upon the bank of a small, but rapid stream, a large and rudely constructed frame building, apparently designed for machinery. It was not yet fully inclosed.

As I looked, I saw a dense smoke arise from the building, and heard the cry of fire from a large number of people.

It seemed that the wind blew strong from the mountain towards the building. The people came up on the opposite side of the building, to put out the fire, and they were blinded by the smoke which blew in their faces. I thought how foolish they were, to thus stay on the opposite side from the wind, to be blinded with the smoke.

Looking, I saw a bucket with a rope attached on a flume through which the water ran. I quickly took it up, drew it full of water, looked for the center of the fire, dashed it in, and, all at once, the flame was extinguished.

I thought a multitude of people came crowding into the building, wondering by whom the fire had been extinguished. Although I was with them, they appeared to comprehend nothing of my agency in the matter. I thought they were almost wild with joy, that the building, although somewhat

charred and damaged, had been saved. They calculated that
the damage the building had sustained was about fifty
thousand dollars.

I awoke in the morning, strangely impressed with the dream.
I related it to Brother Nathan Tanner, who was then with
me. I told him I thought we should see its interpretation.

That morning, Brother Tanner called on one of the native
Saints, who was living with Halalea, one of the highest
native chiefs. He was a special friend of, and a counselor to,
the king, and the man who carried him my letter.

He told Brother Tanner that the king had appointed him
to come with Prince Rehoreho, to meet us that night at our
rooms, lay before us the king's great political trouble, and get
our counsel.

It came plainly to me, then, that therein would be the fulfill-
ment of my dream. About ten o'clock the same evening, they
called on us. They said the king was greatly exercised in his
mind over the troubled condition of his government, and
that he was not decided as to what was best to do.

He said that he could not trust to the counsel of his ministers, nor to the advice of the ministers of other nations then
at his court, for all had some point to gain. Dr. Judd, in his
past troubles, had been his adviser, and, in times of need,
had supplied him with money.

It pained him, then, to turn out of office one who had so
long been his friend, and, upon this subject, he wished us to
give him our wisest counsel.

While Halalea and the prince were delivering their message,
I was continually praying in my heart that the Lord would
give us wisdom to say such things as would do honor to His
cause, for I felt very small for such an important occasion.

After they delivered the king's message in full, I arose and
told them that we were not sent to meddle with governments,
nor to teach political science, but to preach the gospel of
Christ as now revealed. But, inasmuch as the king was our
friend, and desired counsel of us, we would give him such as
the Lord would put in our hearts.

I told them the Bible said, that "when the wicked rule,
the people mourn;" that if Dr. Judd was really a good man

and a true friend to the king, as the king had believed him to be, he would not now allow the king to be in such great trouble on his account, but, like a true friend, would resign his office for the sake of peace between the king and his subjects.

The fact that he was disposed to hold on to his office, at the expense of peace to the king's realm, showed, conclusively, that he was influenced by other motives than the peace and welfare of the kingdom. "We feel," said I, "that the present great political trouble and mourning is owing to Dr. Judd not being a good man, but wickedly holding a grasp upon the government office against the wishes of the people, for which there is no necessity, as the king has many true subjects of more than equal ability, any one of whom he could appoint as Dr. Judd's successor."

When I ceased speaking, the king's messengers clasped my hands and said: "The things you have told us we had not thought of, and they are true. The king will be glad when we tell him what you have said, for we can see it plainly, now. We will assure you that, at ten o'clock to-morrow, you will hear the king's herald proclaiming through the streets of the city that Dr. Judd is removed from office."

They left us with the warmest feelings of gratitude and friendship.

The next morning at ten o'clock, the heralds were heard proclaiming the dismissal of Dr. Judd. The news created wonder and astonishment among the people, and they hurried together with public demonstrations of joy. They greatly marveled and queried by what agency, or through whose influence this long delayed, though most desirable object had been attained.

As I had dreamed, so I saw the people greatly rejoicing, and, although I was daily among them, they had no thought that a Latter-day Saint could have had any agency in so important a matter.

At night the city was brilliantly illuminated. There were few windows in it that did not have, at least, one candle to each pane of glass.

In a settlement with Dr. Judd, as I had dreamed, the government found that it had lost fifty thousand dollars.

Thus my prophecy and my dream were fulfilled together, and peace returned to the people. Joy came to our hearts that the Lord, through the inspiration of His Holy Spirit, had made us, His humble Elders, the means of giving saving counsel to princes.

———•••———

SPECIAL PROVIDENCES.

. ———

CIRCUMSTANCES UNDER WHICH THE EARLY TEMPLES WERE
BUILT—HOW THE WORKMEN WERE ENCOURAGED—AR-
RIVAL OF BROTHER L—— IN NAUVOO—HIS WILLINGNESS
TO WORK WITHOUT PAY—HIS EXTREME WANT—APPEALS
TO GOD FOR HELP—MONEY MIRACULOUSLY PROVIDED—
PRAYER FOR FOOD ANSWERED—PROVIDENTIAL FINDING
OF A PAIR OF SHOES ON THE PLAINS—A CRIPPLED
SHOULDER RESTORED WHILE DEFENDING THE CHARACTER
OF JOSEPH SMITH.

IF a record had been kept of all the facts connected with the building of the Kirtland and Nauvoo Temples, it would tell a curious story of poverty, self-denial, dependence upon God and wants providentially supplied.

No doubt such a record has been kept, but not here on earth. We have not access to it. But many, very many of those who had the privilege of aiding in the work of building those temples have gone to meet that record. Some doubtless will meet it with satisfaction, with joy untold; others with remorse and self-reproach.

Could the Saints of the present day peruse that record, it would put many of them to the blush to think they had done so little in aid of such works. They would see that, though they have enjoyed peace and plenty, they have done almost nothing towards the temples in our day, compared with what the poor Saints did in building those earlier houses of God.

The Kirtland Temple was built when the Saints were few in number and in great poverty, and though comparatively small in size, the erection of such a building by the tithes and voluntary donations of those who were faithful, was a very great undertaking. That it was finished in so short a time was remarkable, and this fact speaks volumes for the devotion of the Saints of that early day.

When the Nauvoo Temple was commenced, the Saints had increased considerably in numbers, but were, as a rule, even poorer than in the days of Kirtland. They had been persecuted by their enemies, driven from their homes and plundered of their property. Finding a temporary rest in a bend of the Mississippi river, a locality noted for its insalubrity, they had struggled in the midst of malarial sickness and severe privations to establish new homes, and had only just begun to gather a few comforts around them when they were required by revelation from the Lord to build a temple to His name.

Upon that temple, many of the Saints labored month after month, with an energy and interest that only religious zeal can impart. They had learned something of the use and importance of temples, before that building was commenced, but as the work advanced more light was given them from time to time. The Prophet of God would visit the workmen and instruct and encourage them in their labors personally, frequently pronouncing blessings upon their heads for their diligence and faithfulness, and when persecution became so strong that he was obliged to hide from his enemies, he sent the written word to stimulate them in their labors, and explained the doctrine of baptism for the dead, then newly revealed.

While living thus in seclusion, he wrote to the Saints in Nauvoo, on the 1st of September, 1842: "And again, verily thus saith the Lord, let the work of my temple, and all the works which I have appointed unto you, be continued on and not cease; and let your diligence, and your perseverance, and patience, and your works be redoubled, and you shall in nowise lose your reward, saith the Lord of hosts. And if they persecute you, so persecuted they the prophets and righteous men that were before you. For all this there is a reward in heaven."

Again, on the 6th of the same month, he wrote additional words of encouragement, unfolding still farther that glorious saving principle as it had been revealed to him, and roused the workmen to action by this stirring appeal: "Brethren, shall we not go on in so great a cause? Go forward and not backward. Courage, brethren; and on, on to the victory! Let your hearts rejoice, and be exceeding glad. Let the earth break forth into singing. Let the dead speak forth anthems of eternal praise to the King Immanuel, who hath ordained before the world was, that which would enable us to redeem them out of their prison; for the prisoners shall go free."

Being thus encouraged, and knowing that the time allowed for building the house was limited, the men worked with a will and determination that made success certain. Though they had to stand guard at night to prevent their enemies from surprising the city during the darkness and slaying its defenseless inhabitants, they did not cease their exertions during the daytime to erect the house of God. Though they went on short rations till some of them actually fainted beside their work, from sheer hunger and exhaustion, still they persevered. Though the mechanics employed upon the temple had tempting offers of abundant work and ready pay if they would go outside of Nauvoo and labor, many of them preferred to remain and work without pecuniary reward in rearing that sacred structure.

The case of one of those workmen will serve to illustrate the self-sacrificing disposition manifested by many of those who labored upon that building, as well as the way their simple wants were sometimes supplied by the Almighty.

Brother L—— arrived in Nauvoo from England, his native country, in March, 1844. He was an excellent mechanic, had held good situations and been in good circumstances in the "old country," and his skill as a workman was such as to command ready employment and high wages in any of the large cities of America, had such been his object.

But he had embraced the gospel and received a testimony of its truth, and afterwards the spirit of gathering with the Saints, which enabled him to brook the taunts and ridicule heaped upon him by friends and relatives for his unpopular faith, and resist the pleading of aged parents, who were loath to part with him.

His faith and zeal were such that he had left friends and property and all that he had formerly held dear, and come to America that he might be with the chosen people of God and assist in building up Zion.

He was ambitious to labor upon the temple, and applied for work immediately upon his arrival in Nauvoo. When informed that there was plenty of work but nothing to pay with, he replied that pay was no consideration.

He took hold with a determination, and worked with all the energy with which the young, strong and enthusiastic nature was capable from that time until the work upon the temple ceased, upwards of two years, and during that time only received in cash for his services the small amount of fifty cents.

Many a time he felt the pangs of hunger, and went to his work fasting rather than join with his family in eating the last ration of food in their possession, but the Lord sustained him by His Spirit, gave him joy in his labors and provided a way for more food to be obtained to sustain the lives of himself and family.

He and his young wife had a habit of appealing to the Almighty in prayer when in an extremity, and they invariably found comfort in so doing, and generally had their prayers answered.

Upon one occasion, their infant child was dangerously sick, and they felt the want of twenty-five cents to procure some medicine with. Where to get it they did not know, and so, as usual, they prayed to the Lord to open their way to obtain it. They felt an assurance on arising from their knees that their prayer would be answered, but they knew not how. Soon afterwards the husband happened to feel some hard substance in the waistband of his pants, and called his wife's attention to it, wondering what it could be. The pants were almost new. They had been made to order for him only a short time before. There was no hole in the band, and it seemed that, whatever it was, it must have been inserted between the pieces of cloth when the pants were being made, and yet he thought it strange that he had not discovered it before.

To solve the mystery, a few stitches were cut, and the waistband opened, when, lo! there were two new ten cent pieces and one five cent piece—just the amount of money they required to buy medicine with.

Lest the money might have been lost by the tailor who made the pants, a very poor man who lived neighbor to them, he took it to him and asked him, but that impecunious individual said he knew it could not be his, for he had never had a cent of money in his possession for months.

They accepted it as a gift from the Lord, bought the medicine their child needed and he was soon well.

When the work on the temple was nearing completion, the food supply for the family became entirely exhausted, and there seemed no prospect of obtaining any more without quitting the work on the temple and going elsewhere for employment. That, of course, Brother L—— was averse to doing, and in this, as in other cases of extremity, he and his wife retired to their bedroom to lay the matter before the Lord. They had scarcely finished their prayer when a knock was heard at the door. On opening it, they found a man there who said he desired a particular job of work done, which he did not feel like entrusting to anyone else but Brother L——. However, he was in no particular hurry for it, it need not be done till the work on the temple was completed, but he wanted to arrange and pay for it then, as he was going on a foreign mission. "But," said he, "I have nothing to pay you for it but wheat; can you use that?"

It was the very thing the family stood most in need of; it was gratefully accepted and regarded as a direct answer to their prayer, and within a short time the wheat was ground and a good supply of flour returned from it.

When the Saints were preparing to leave Nauvoo, wagons for the journey were in great demand, and every person among them who had ever worked at wagon-making, and very many also who never had, set to work making them. Good timber was tolerably plentiful, but iron cost cash, and that was a scarce article. All sorts of nonedescript vehicles were hastily improvised, many of them so rude in their construction as ·to put the veriest bungler of a wheelwright to · the blush for their appearance. Yet under the blessing of God they did good service. Some of them, for the want of iron, were made almost entirely of wood. In some extreme cases they were even made without the usual iron tires, strips of rawhide being nailed on the felloes as a substitute. One, at least, of the wagons made in this fashion stood the trip across the plains, and was used for several years after its arrival in Salt Lake Valley.

Brother L—— had been fortunate enough to get the wood work of a wagon made, but how to procure the iron was a question which greatly perplexed him. However, he knew that he was engaged in the Lord's service, and he felt that he had a claim upon His mercy and blessings. Accordingly, he and his wife made their want a subject of earnest prayer, and then went on about their duties, trusting in the Lord to answer their petition.

Soon afterwards Brother L—— had occasion to go out on the prairie in search of his cow, which had strayed off, and during his absence encountered a drenching shower, so that when he returned home he found it necessary to change his clothing. He hung his wet clothes before a fire in the open fireplace to dry, and as he did so a bright gold sovereign, a ten and a five cent piece dropped to the floor, apparently from his pocket. He knew, however, that he had no money previously, and he could account for its presence there only by its having been sent by the Lord. It was the exact amount required to purchase the iron for his wagon, and it was soon obtained and the wagon finished.

With such manifestations as these of God's goodness, he was encouraged to continue in his labors upon the temple of God, and when it was so far completed that the holy ordinances for which it was designed could be performed in it, he felt repaid in the blessings which he therein received for all his efforts towards its construction.

A rather remarkable case of special providence occurred when Brother L—— was crossing the plains, coming to Salt Lake Valley. His shoes gave out, and his feet became very sore from having to walk so much while driving his ox team, etc. Early one morning, when he, in company with another brother, were out hunting for their cattle, he exclaimed to his companion as he limped and hobbled over the rocky ground, "Oh! I do wish the Lord would send me a pair of shoes!"

He had not walked many rods after expressing this wish when he saw something lying a short distance ahead of him, and called the attention of his companion to it, who remarked that it must be the bell and strap lost off one of the oxen, but to the inexpressible joy of Brother L——, he found, on approaching the object, that it was a new pair of shoes, which had evidently never been worn, and which he found, on trying them on, to fit him as well as if they had been made for him. He thanked the Lord for them, for he felt that it was through His merciful providence that they had been left there, and went on his way rejoicing. The shoes did him good service.

While alluding to Brother L——, another incident may be related from his experience to illustrate the manner in which the Almighty sustains and blesses those who are valiant in defending His cause and the character of His anointed servants.

At an early period in the settlement of Salt Lake Valey, Brother L—— had a severe attack of inflammatory rl eumatism and bilious fever, from which he suffered a long time, and which drew his shoulder out of place and left him in a very helpless condition. He was in that fix for about six months—able to walk about, but unable to make any use whatever of one arm. He could not even dress himself. Surgeons examined his shoulder, and assured him that it was out of joint, and urged him to have it set. He, however, declined accepting their advice, as he had faith that the Lord would make him whole in answer to his prayer.

Living neighbor to him in Salt Lake City, and holding an office to which he had been appointed by the vote of the members of the Ward, was a man by the name of Gallup, who was a rank apostate at heart, although he had a standing in the Church.

In conversation with Brother L—— one day, this man Gallup advocated the doctrines of a certain man named Gladden Bishop, who had once belonged to the Church but who had apostatized and attempted to start a church of his own.

Brother L—— became so disgusted with his false reasoning and bitter, malignant spirit that he went to the Bishop of the Ward and made complaint about such a man as Gallup being allowed to hold an office in the Ward or even a membership in the Church.

The result was, a Priesthood meeting was called, and Mr. Gallup was cited to appear and state his views upon the subject of religion.

In the course of his speech he declared: "Joseph Smith was a wicked and adulterous man; he ate and drank with the drunkard, his lot was cast with the hypocrite and unbeliever, and he has gone to hell."

This was too much for Brother L—— to stand, even in his crippled condition. He could not tamely submit to hear the character of a man assailed whom he loved dearer than his life. Jumping to his feet and springing over the benches that stood between him and Mr. Gallup, he made for him with the intention of administering summary vengeance. Several persons immediately interposed to prevent him from inflicting any bodily injury upon Gallup, and it was noticed that he made use of his crippled arm, and when the excitement subsided he discovered himself that his shoulder had assumed its natural position and that he was as well as he ever had been.

Gallup, of course, was cut off from the Church, and thought himself fortunate, no doubt, in escaping a castigation, and Brother L—— went home rejoicing, and entered his house swinging his arm which had been so long useless and shouting for joy, while his wife wept tears of gratitude for the good-u ss of God in bringing about his restoration to health and soundness.

———— • • • ————

INCIDENTS ON THE PLAINS.

BY A. M. C.

CHAPTER I.

ARMY SENT TO UTAH—MISSIONARIES CALLED HOME—LARGE NUMBER ASSEMBLE AT FLORENCE—DANGERS OF THE TRIP—COUNCIL TO DECIDE UPON COURSE OF ACTION— FORTUNATE FOG—PROVIDENTIAL STORM.

IN 1857, James Buchanan, who was then President of the United States, sent an army to this Territory, for the purpose, it was said, of punishing the "Mormons" for breaking the laws and doing violence to the judges who had been sent here.

This was the excuse given for the army being sent; but the people of the Territory had not violated the laws nor done any injury to any of the officers of the Government; they were then, as they ever have been, peaceable and law abiding.

The real object for sending the troops here, was to crush out what the world called "Mormonism."

The principal men who urged the sending of troops here, were traitors in their hearts against the Government, and they hoped by taking these steps to divert the attention of the country from their own wicked schemes; and also to get the army of the United States out of the way by having it sent to this distant region. By accomplishing this, they thought they could operate to advantage in bringing about their own designs.

The army was kept out at Fort Bridger all that winter and many of the officers and soldiers were very angry because they could not come into our cities and enjoy themselves at our expense.

When it was found that the army was marching here, and there was likely to be trouble, the Elders in Europe and in the United States were re-called; but feelings ran so high in the United States against our people that it was somewhat dangerous for a man to travel and be known as a "Mormon." On the plains there were men on the watch for every one bearing the name of Latter-day Saint.

It was under these circumstances that the Elders assembled at the frontiers to return home. One hundred and ten of them crossed the Missouri river in the beginning of May, 1858, at the point formerly known as Winter Quarters; at present it is called Florence.

They were anxious to get home, some of them having been absent a year and others for three or four years.

There were, in reality, two companies; one composed of Elders returning from the United States and Canada, Elder David Brinton being their captain, and the Elders returning from Europe, who had Elder John W. Berry as their captain. It was deemed advisable, however, in view of the troubled and uncertain state of affairs, for both companies to travel together.

The writer was in the company of Elders returning from the United States, where he had been on a mission for upwards of three years.

We had heard of several of our brethren being taken by the army and held under threats, and we knew not what our fate would be were the soldiers to get us in their power; for they accused every Latter-day Saint of treachery to the Government while they themselves were in reality the traitors as the sebsequent careers of many of them fully proved.

Many thought that, as the roads were all blocked, and carefully watched by the troops, when we came in the vicinity of the army we would be under the necessity of burning or abandoning our wagons and everything that we could not pack on our animals.

Among the brethren was a man whose name was Pope; he had a wife and two or three small children. They were very anxious to accompany us, and, although the perils we were about to encounter were of a serious nature, they could not be induced by anything that could be said to them to remain behind. A council of the Elders was held upon their case, and it was agreed to permit Brother Pope to accompany us, as well as four brethren who proposed walking the entire distance to the Valley.

It was a time that required faith to be exercised, for the affairs of the Saints were in a critical condition. We knew, however, that God had delivered us when we had relied upon Him, and we united with great zeal in imploring His blessing, that He might overrule everything in such a manner that we could return in safety to the society of our families and friends.

After leaving Winter Quarters we traveled on without interruption until we drew near to Fort Kearny. Our road was on the north side of the Platte, and Fort Kearny was on the south side. There were troops at the fort, and they were on the alert to prevent companies of men or any kind of aid passing over the road to help the "Mormons" in Utah; for they pretended to look upon our people as public enemies.

It was our custom at such times to hold a council, and take into consideration the best course to pursue. The Elders all came together and we prayed to the Lord, and asked Him to bestow upon us His Holy Spirit and to lead and guide us in our operations. When we unitedly decided in council upon pursuing a certain course we always felt that that was the mind and will of the Lord unto us.

It was decided at this council that we should avoid attracting the attention of the people of the fort by passing it in the night.

Unfortunately, as it seemed at the time, it rained heavily that evening and we were only able to travel until a little past midnight. By that time ourselves and our animals were so thoroughly fatigued and the night was so dark that we were compelled to stop and tie up for the night.

. Our reflections were not very pleasant, because we felt sure that when morning dawned upon us we would be in full sight of the fort, and undoubtedly would receive a visit from the officers and troops.

We awoke with the dawn of day, and instead of being able to see the fort, or its occupants being able to see us, we found our camp enveloped in a fog, the mist being so dense that it was with difficulty we could see each other. We taveled on in the fog until afternoon, by which time we were out of sight of the fort.

After leaving this point we had plenty of game, buffalo, antelope, etc., and we were able to obtain an abundance of fresh meat, which made this part of the journey exceedingly pleasant; for though in an Indian country, we had not the fear of the wild and savage red men that we had of those of our own color, who professed to be the loyal citizens of our government.

As we approached the junction of the North and South Platte, a herd of mules passed us. They were being driven in the direction of Fort Laramie and were traveling at a much faster gait than we were going. The men who were driving them saw us, and we fully expected they would carry the intelligence to the fort of our being close by. It was known that "Mormon" Elders were returning to the Valley, and the military were prepared to stop them, or to otherwise interfere with them.

When within half a day's travel of Fort Laramie, another council was called to take into consideration the best course to pursue. We settled the matter by determining to rest on Sunday, rise early the following morning and pass the fort in daylight, as we felt satisfied the troops were informed of our approach by the men who had just passed us.

Monday was a beautiful day; we traveled on without interruption until we came in sight of the fort, which was about one o'clock, when one of the severest hailstorms any of us had ever seen broke upon us. The hail fell so rapidly that our animals could scarcely travel on account of their feet balling up with it. Our train had been seen from the fort and parties had started to meet us; but when the storm broke upon them, they were compelled to retreat to their quarters. The storm was too severe for them to remain out in it.

I learned afterwards that when the storm ceased a company of men had been sent from Fort Laramie to overtake us. They followed us as far as the North Platte bridge, and not being able to reach us at this point, they deemed it best to return again to the fort. We were not aware of this at the time; but having traveled leisurely from Kearny to Laramie, our animals were in much better condition than when we started; and fearing that the people at Laramie might make some attempt to stop us, we made forced drives until we reached Independence Rock on the Sweetwater. Thus the Lord again delivered us from the hands of our enemies in a most providential manner; for had it not been for this hailstorm it is altogether likely we would have been stopped.

CHAPTER II.

APOSTATES MET—THE CHAPLAIN SEPARATES FROM THE COMPANY TO MEET SOME APOSTATES—AN ADVENTUROUS TRIP—DISCHARGED GOVERNMENT TEAMSTERS INDIGNANT AT "MORMONS"—PLOT TO STEAL THE CHAPLAIN'S HORSE—ADVICE TO THE APOSTATES TO LOOK TO THEIR OWN SAFETY — MR. STOUT'S COMPASSION FOR THE HATCHET-FACED MISSOURIAN—HOW HIS CONFIDENCE WAS REWARDED — MEET CAPTAIN HATCH—NEWS OF BUCHANAN'S AMNESTY PROCLAMATION — EVADE THE ARMY, AND REACH THE VALLEY SAFELY.

AT the Three Crossings of the Sweetwater we met a company of apostates, who were in full retreat from the Valley, unwilling to trust God's providence to screen them from the wrath of our enemies, and anxious to get back to the States.

The night following we encamped at the eastern end of what is known as the Seminole cut-off. The company intended to travel on this cut-off in the morning.

That evening the chaplain of our company, a young Elder who had a fondness for adventure, proposed that he should travel on the old route, for the purpose of meeting a man for whom he had transacated some business in the States, and who, he was informed, was returning in a company of apostates. Captains Berry and Brinton thought he ought not to attempt to go by that route alone ; at this, one of the other Elders volunteered to accompany him. But when morning came the latter had changed his mind; for it had stormed during the night, snow had fallen and it still snowed very hard, and he thought the weather too disagreeable for so lonely a trip.

Mr. Chaplain, however, in opposition to all remonstrances, was resolved to go, and he started out alone, on horseback, taking with him some blankets and a few crackers. It was the eleventh day of June—a strange time, you would think, for snow to fall, yet it continued to descend until the middle of the afternoon, and was so deep that when he came to a place on the Sweetwater, called the Rocky Ridge, he was obliged to dismount and lead his pony. It was a lonely trip which he took, and through a wild, desolate country; it was with considerable pleasure, therefore, that he came in sight of the camp which he sought just as the sun was going down.

It was encamped on what is known as Quaking-Aspen Creek. The man whom he expected to meet was not in the company; but he found others whom he had known, persons who did not love the gospel sufficiently to endure the trials promised to the Saints; but were desirous to return to that Babylon from which they had been gathered.

When the chaplain rejoined his companions, the Elders, he related the incidents of this trip and I was permitted to take the following account from his journal:

"I had just staked my animal to feed upon the brush in the neighborhood of the camp, when a company of discharged Government teamsters passed by on their way east, under the guidance of George Merrick. On account of the hardships they had endured the previous winter, they were very indignant at everybody called 'Mormon.' They had calculated on enjoying themselves at our people's expense in the Valley; but instead of that, they had been kept out all winter, and they were disappointed. An hour later one Ephraim Thornton, a young man who, when a boy, in Nauvoo, had been a schoolmate of mine, but who was now an apostate, took me aside and informed me of a plan which had been arranged to rob me of my horse. A discharged Government teamster had sworn to take it, or die in the attempt.

"I thanked Mr. Thornton for the information; but I advised him to have the camp look to their own affairs, and I would conduct mine, adding that I did not fear that teamster's threats, as 'barking dogs seldom bite.'

"There was one Mr. Stout in this company, with whom I conversed. He was bound for the States, and was accompanied by his wife. He told me that he had been successful in raising stock in Cedar Valley, and had sold them for the gold to the army he had just passed at Fort Bridger. He pointed out to me a young hatchet-faced Missourian, with long hair and snake-like appearance, whom he represented as a Government teamster, a poor fellow for whom he felt compassion, and whom he was carrying to his home. It was vain for me to advise him not to trust Mr. Hatchet-face too far. He had confidence in him; I had none; I would not have trusted him out of my sight. My views in relation to him received speedy confirmation; for while standing with my back to the fire looking in the direction of my pony, I heard Mr. Stout swear very hard at his wife for leaving the wagon. His sack of gold, amounting to $1.500 had disappeared. An investigation revealed the fact that not only was the gold missing, but crackers, blankets, several watches and other things, besides a race mare belonging to one Joseph Greenwood, were all gone, and with them the poor fellow, the Missourian, for whom Mr. Stout had felt so much compassion! It afterwards transpired that he had been making his arrangements for flight for several days. My advice to Mr. Thornton for the camp to look to their own affairs was very timely, as this transaction proved.

"That my horse might not be stolen I made my bed upon the snow, holding the bridle in my hand, and my pistols ready for use in my belt. But I was undisturbed. I arose in the morning and left the camp and its misery to continue my journey towards the home of our people. As I left the last crossing of the Sweetwater and was ascending the South Pass, I met a company of our brethren, under Captain Abram Hatch, going to the North Platte on business. It was fortunate that I took this route, for they had word for our company which, had I not met them, we would not have received. Upon learning where the Elders were, they turned and accompanied me. We found the company on the cut-off, five miles from its junction with the old road."

Our chaplain seemed happy at rejoining us, and from his wearied looks and blistered face, we judged he would not soon go again in search of apostates. But, as he said in his journal, it was fortunate that he had taken that route. The providence of the Lord was in it, and it was overruled for our good by his meeting Captain Hatch and companions. They brought us President Buchanan's amnesty proclamation, which was read, also the intelligence of our people's move

South : also instructions from President Young to the effect that unless otherwise instructed, we were to take the Sublet cut-off to the north until we struck Bear river, and then travel on the trail which would lead us to the head of Echo canyon.

From Captain Hatch, also, we learned that it was the intention of Col. Albert Sidney Johnson, the commander of the army, to leave Fort Bridger the following Monday for the Valley.

But little remains to be said of our journey home after parting with Captain Abram Hatch and companions. We had reached the Big Bend on the Sandy, when we found that we had passed the Sublet cut-off and were where the Kinney cut-off led north. It was decided in council to travel on that route.

We soon struck Green river, and as if Providence had arranged affairs for us, we found a fine ferry boat tied at the river side, upon which we crossed. We continued to travel by this route from this point to Bear river, which we crossed in our wagon boxes, there being no boat, and swam our horses. Bear river not being very wide, we had no difficulty in crossing by this means.

We came into Echo canyon twelve miles west of Yellow creek. From mountaineers whom some of the Elders met, and who were going east with supplies to meet the army, we learned that Johnson and the army were encamped that night on Yellow creek. They also informed the brethren that a company of two hundred and fifty sappers and miners were ahead of us, reparing the road and removing obstructions before the advance of the army.

We overtook this company next morning. Had they suspected that we had not been seen by the main army, they would very likely have stopped us. But they had no idea that we had come by any other route, and therefore after asking us how far back the command was, the order was given, "Clear the road, boys, and let them pass." From this point we traveled on until we reached Salt Lake City without meeting any incident worthy of note.